Violence in Schools

Learning in Fear

Violence in Schools
Learning in Fear

Nancy Day

—Issues in Focus—

ENSLOW PUBLISHERS, INC.

44 Fadem Road	P.O. Box 38
Box 699	Aldershot
Springfield, N.J. 07081	Hants GU12 6BP
U.S.A.	U.K.

Library of Congress Cataloging-in-Publication Data

Day, Nancy.
    Violence in schools : learning in fear / Nancy Day.
        p. cm. — (Issues in focus)
    Includes bibliographical references (p.   ) and index.
    Summary: Examines the increasing acts of violence and vandalism committed at
school by students and others.
    ISBN 0-89490-734-4
    1. School violence—United States—Juvenile literature. 2. School
vandalism—United States—Juvenile literature. [1. School violence. 2. School
vandalism.] I. Title. II. Series: Issues in focus (Hillside, N.J.)
LB3013.3.D39 1996
371.5'8—dc20   95-40198
                                                    CIP
                                                    AC

Printed in the United States of America

10 9 8 7 6 5 4 3 2

Contents

All our efforts to raise the standard of American education will be to no avail unless we provide children with a safe and disciplined environment that is conducive to learning.

—U.S. Secretary of Education Richard Riley[1]

1

Learning in Fear

It was the week before spring break. Alex Orange, a popular student and football player at West Charlotte High School in Charlotte, North Carolina, was looking forward to spending time with his dad in Tennessee. But that Friday, he decided to stop by a house party being held by the Debonairs, a West Charlotte social club. It had been billed as a "Stop the Violence Jam." Alex, who never carried a gun and kept out of trouble, planned to meet his friend Angie Bynum there.

As often happens, word of the party spread. School would be out soon, and students were ready to celebrate. More than two hundred teenagers were dancing, talking, and having fun, when some students from a rival high school showed up looking for trouble. They began beating people with baseball bats. Then Alex Orange saw a man pull out a gun. He grabbed it, but when he lost his grip, the man pointed the gun at him and fired, blasting a hole in his chest. People began to run.

Just then, Alex's friend Angie Bynum drove up. She remembers it was pure chaos. "We stopped a guy and said, 'What happened? What happened?' He told us that Alex Orange had been killed. And I just went 'NO!'"

Angie found her friend on the porch. He was dead. "It was like a bad dream," Bynum recalls. "I couldn't believe it had happened." She rushed to the house where Alex's mom lived so she could break the news gently. It was too late. "We could hear the gospel music playing and we knew she knew her son was dead."[2]

Crime Comes to School

"I want you to stop the killing in the city," wrote nine-year-old James Darby to President Bill Clinton. "I think someone might kill me. I'm asking you nicely to stop it. I know you can do it." Nine days later, James was shot in the head during a drive-by shooting and died. President Clinton had not been able to stop the violence James Darby seemed to know would claim him.[3]

Unfortunately, what happened to James Darby is not unusual. Homicide is the third-leading cause of death for children between the ages of ten and twenty-four. And it is the leading killer of African Americans, both male and female, between fifteen and thirty-four.[4]

People are at the greatest risk of being crime victims during their teenage years. In 1992, almost one in every four violent crimes involved a victim aged twelve to seventeen.[5] Teenagers are more than twice as likely to be victims of violent crime than those over twenty.[6] It is not surprising, then, that some of those crimes take place in schools. The National Institute of Education found that children between the ages of twelve and nineteen run greater risk of being a victim of crime in school than out, in part because 50 percent of those arrested for a crime in America are teenagers.[7]

How big is the problem? In the time it took you to read to this point in the book, fifteen school crimes were committed. (A school crime occurs every six seconds.)[8] More than 3 million crimes—about 11 percent of the total number of crimes committed in the United States each year—occur in schools.[9]

School is no longer a safe haven for children. Over 7 percent of students report that they have been threatened or injured with a weapon, and over 16 percent have been in a physical fight on school property during the past twelve months. One third of students have had property stolen or deliberately damaged on school property during the past year.[10] Four percent of white students and 11 percent of African-American students report having been threatened with a gun at least once in the last month.[11] Violence is now the second-leading cause of death among students.[12]

School violence is a growing problem. Students were killed or seriously injured as a result of school violence in 41 percent of America's large cities surveyed by the National League of Cities. Of seven hundred cities surveyed, 38 percent said there had been a noticeable increase in school violence in the past five years. Only 17 percent said violence had gone down or was not a problem. One fourth of the cities reported school violence-related student deaths or injuries that required hospitalization within the previous year.[13] Students no longer feel safe at school. In the United States, 4.4 percent of students missed at least one day of school during the last thirty days because they felt unsafe at school or felt unsafe traveling to or from school.[14] Yet the problem is even larger than these statistics indicate. U.S. Department of Justice surveys consistently indicate that only one third of all crime is reported, and an even smaller number of gang-related crimes are reported.[15]

Many incidents in schools are treated as disciplinary problems and are not reported as crimes. Those that are reported may be downplayed to minimize their seriousness. Students do not want to get into trouble by reporting incidents. Teachers feel pressure to cover up problems to avoid the appearance that they cannot control their classrooms. Even teachers who have been victimized themselves have remained silent, fearful that a violent incident will be a blot on their record.

A study conducted by the National Institute of Education found that two thirds of assaults requiring medical attention were not reported to police by school officials.[16] Schools fear negative publicity and worry that they will get a bad reputation. Other reasons schools do not report incidents include fear that the perpetrator or friends of the perpetrator will seek revenge, the feeling that nothing can be done to stop the problem, fear of being sued, and embarrassment.[17]

Schools are the focal point for other types of crime as well. Burglary rates of schools are five times the burglary rates of businesses and schools are frequently the targets of vandalism and arson as well.[18] While much of the violence in schools is student against student, it can also be student against teacher or teacher against student.

Schools seem to have become magnets for certain types of crime. For example, although teens spend only 25 percent of their waking hours at school, 40 percent of teenage robberies occur there.[19] Robbery is a major crime. Robbers, unlike vandals, thieves, or burglars, confront their victims and use force to commit the crime. J. Edgar Hoover, legendary director of the Federal Bureau of Investigation (FBI), once called robbery "death looking for a place to happen."[20]

School officials agree that not only has school violence increased, but the incidents have become more serious. A survey conducted by the National School Boards Association found that 93 percent of the urban school districts, 81 percent of the suburban districts, and 69 percent of the rural districts responding had experienced student assaults on students. Among urban districts responding to the survey, 39 percent had experienced a shooting or knifing, 23 percent a drive-by shooting, and 15 percent a rape.[21] The perpetrators are getting younger (one fourth of all suspensions for violent incidents are elementary-school students) and the crimes are getting more serious (arrests of juveniles for murder rose 85 percent between 1987 and 1991).[22]

In 1985, the National School Boards Association identified characteristics of schools with the highest levels of student victimization. The schools tended to be located in urban poverty-stricken areas with high unemployment and crime. They had students who tested low on ability tests and had a high level of absenteeism, and they had a high percentage of parents who were welfare recipients. The schools that experienced higher levels of victimization of both students and teachers were schools with high proportions of students who read below grade level and high percentages of minority students. School crime increased with school size and class size and was also related to whether teachers had enough access to the materials needed for teaching.[23]

Not all school violence is caused by students. Outsiders (students from other schools, students who have been expelled, or adults) go into schools to rob, attack, kidnap, rape, or murder students or staff members. This can occur when an outsider wants to harm a specific individual. For example, a gang member may seek revenge on someone who happens to be a student and attack him or her at school. Or violence can occur when one person attacks another at random on school grounds. For example, a drug addict may enter a school to rob or steal and may assault a teacher or student.

It is important to remember that school crime affects more than just the victim and the perpetrator. It affects the whole school. Students may become fearful, angry, and frustrated. They may feel guilty that they were not able to prevent the incident, and they may even suffer long-term psychological problems. Like an adult whose home has been burglarized, students may feel violated. Their sense of security may be damaged, possibly never to be fully repaired.

Violence is a complicated issue that will not be resolved by any one solution, but students, teachers, school officials, police officers, and community leaders are all searching for answers. Across the country, hundreds of different programs are in place in an attempt to stop school violence. Some are educational programs put on by schools, some are community-based solutions, and others

Dawne Orange, Alex's mother, campaigns against teen violence.

are directed by the students themselves, who realize that unless they do something, they too may learn James Darby's painful lesson—nobody is safe if we do not stop the killing.

Alex's Legacy

The Monday after Alex Orange's killing, West Charlotte High staff members told students that there would be a meeting to discuss what had happened. That day, two hundred fifty students showed up, but they did not just cry, and they did not just express their anger. They *did* something.

Angie Bynum was the one who pointed the way. "I stood up and said 'This is not fair,'" recalls Bynum. "'It's not right.'" There had to be more to it. Alex should not be forgotten. She suggested they start something like SADD (Students Against Drunk Driving), only called SAV (Students Against Violence). Another student added, "Not just here at West Charlotte. It should be everywhere." So they came up with SAVE (Students Against Violence Everywhere).

Angie Bynum had to grow up fast. For Angie, like others who have lost loved ones to violence, the pain has not gone away.

> Nobody my age had ever died before in my life. I had a lot of questions and I had a lot of anger and I'm glad my anger came out in positiveness. It's something that someone else can benefit from. What I want to do is save the next student from having to go through this, burying a friend; save the next parent like Dawne [Alex Orange's mother] from having years and years of having to miss your child. . . . I don't care what people say, you don't get over it. The hurt doesn't go anywhere. You still remember.[24]

You can get a gun on the street, you can get it from drug dealers. It's easy as getting a loaf of bread.

—a girl incarcerated for committing a violent crime[1]

2

From Chewing Gum to Toting Guns

Some people look back with fondness on the "good old days," when the worst thing a trouble-making student might do was to chew gum in class or stick a girl's pigtails in an inkwell. Now, it seems, the student is more likely to threaten a classmate with a gun or stab a student in a stairwell. Has the situation really changed that dramatically? If so, why?

When searching for reasons that explain the problem of school violence, many people point the finger at society. A survey of school board members, for example, cited the breakdown of the family and violence in the media as the two leading causes of school violence, followed by alcohol and drug abuse, easy access to guns, and poverty.[2] Is society to blame? Bad parenting? TV violence? Or is some biological factor at work? Researchers are struggling to find answers.

How We Got Here

Concerned citizens gathered in Philadelphia to discuss the problem of teenage gangs. The public had become increasingly concerned about crime in their community, particularly among juveniles. The citizens wanted to know what had gone wrong with these young people and what could be done to stop them.[3] The citizens might have watched Bill Moyer's television special on youth violence to learn more, except that it would not be on for more than two hundred years. In fact, television would not be invented for another 135 years. The year was 1791. George Washington was president and Abraham Lincoln had not even been born.

Gangs have existed since the 1700s. The first gangs were mainly social clubs. Although they often vandalized property, they rarely attacked people. Then, after World War II, gang members began using weapons such as knives and zip guns (crude, homemade pistols). Fights or "rumbles" became common as the gangs grew in the 1950s and 1960s.

Nevertheless, school violence was not a major concern. A 1956 survey by the National Education Association reported that two thirds of the responding teachers said that fewer than one percent of their students caused disturbances or disruptions. Students were described as exceptionally well behaved or reasonably well behaved by 95 percent of the teachers.[4]

During the late 1960s and early 1970s, gang activity dropped. Rebellious youths were more likely to become involved in political protest. Then, in the mid- to late-1970s, a new burst of gang activity and juvenile crime began.[5] In 1975, arrests of people under age eighteen topped 2 million.[6] Gang activity increased again in the 1980s and continues to rise.

Since the 1970s, youth arrests have actually dropped. In 1992, just under 2 million young people were arrested, even though the United States population grew from just over 200 million in 1970 to almost 250 million in 1990. Juveniles accounted for 16 percent of all arrests in 1992, down from 26 percent in 1970.[7]

Although the percentage of youth arrests is lower, the youth murder rate is much higher, due at least in part to the availability of guns. Young people are also increasingly committing vicious crimes in a casual way, without conscience or concern. Many young people seem to have accepted violence as a way of life. For example, a survey found that 20 percent of high school students at a suburban school saw nothing wrong with shooting someone who had stolen from them.[8]

One explanation is the desperate lives some young people lead. Judge Susan Larabee of the Bronx Family Court in New York states her view:

> The kids I see come from such violent homes and backgrounds. They may have a brother or two in jail for a violent crime. There may be mental illness in the family. There has probably been domestic violence. They may have had a father or mother shot or murdered. Many of these kids are already third-generation violent offenders. Their whole lives are surrounded by violence.[9]

Violence Beyond the Cities

A student, angry because he was not allowed to graduate, kills his former history teacher and three students. An overcrowded, inner-city school in New York or Philadelphia? No—it happened in Olivehurst, California, a rural town of about ten thousand people.[10]

School crime is no longer simply an urban problem. In a 1993 survey, 45 percent of rural school districts reported finding weapons in school and 69 percent had experienced student assaults on students.[11] Rural schools often do not address the problems of school violence because they have an "it can't happen here" attitude. While it is true that the number of crimes is generally lower in rural schools, problems are increasing, and no school is immune.

One problem is that families are increasingly mobile. Even in small towns, people move in and out. A violent student may show up for school, having transferred from another school system or even another state. The new school knows nothing about past incidents involving the student. Even if the violent student lives in the community, privacy laws may prevent social service organizations and law enforcement officials from letting the school know about the student's background.

Violence also occurs in suburban areas. Heather Thompson attended high school in an affluent area of Redmond, Washington. "It was the type of school where you didn't really expect there to be any difficulties," she says. Nevertheless, there were racial fights in which kids ended up with broken noses and other injuries. Thompson also discovered that several of her friends had been raped but had not reported it. When students told a guest speaker from Mothers Against Violence In America that there were no problems in Redmond, she could not believe it. "I was really personally very offended," she recalls. Thompson decided to take a stand against violence. She says that people must realize that violence exists in affluent areas.

> What I always say is that it grows and it breeds under the blanket of the ignorance in those communities . . . people would like to prefer that it's not there. But I've met the mothers and the fathers and the grandmothers and the brothers and the sisters of all these kids that have been brutally murdered. And it changes your life.[12]

Home Life

The American family has changed too. Currently, 57 percent of children under the age of six have two working parents or a single parent.[13] Although having working parents generally means that a child has less parental supervision, it is also a necessity for many families. While lack of supervision can contribute to young people getting into trouble, it certainly is not the only factor. Family problems such as divorce, family violence, drug abuse, poverty, unemployment, and illness all have significant effects on children. In addition, many children are victims of child abuse, which can lead to violent behavior in the future.

Poverty has become a major problem. Currently, 20 percent of students live below the poverty level, compared with 15 percent in 1970.[14] The desperately poor conditions in which some children are growing up has created a subculture with its own ideas of right and wrong. An East Harlem principal, whose student was accused of taking part in the attack and rape of a jogger in New York's Central Park, says that the difference between middle or working class children and poor children is that the ones from comfortable surroundings see violence as a necessary way to temporarily conform, whereas poor children see it as the way the world is.[15]

In *The Anatomy of Human Destructiveness,* psychoanalyst Erich Fromm found that people who have experienced extreme powerlessness in childhood sometimes get pleasure from having life-and-death control over others. In cases where "there is an atmosphere of dullness and joylessness, the child freezes up; there is nothing upon which he can make a dent, nobody who responds or even listens, the child is left with a sense of powerlessness and impotence."[16]

Although a bad childhood does not always cause a sadistic personality, it can contribute to it. Psychoanalyst Heinz Kohut has said that when the child's emotional needs are neglected and no recognition is given for achievement or love, the result can be "narcissistic rage" in adulthood. He describes this rage as "The need for revenge, for righting a wrong, for undoing a hurt by whatever means, and a deeply anchored, unrelenting compulsion in the pursuit of all these aims."[17]

According to the American Psychological Association (APA), the strongest predictor of future violence is a history of violence, including being a victim of abuse. Roughly 70 percent of the men who come through the criminal justice system were abused or neglected as children.[18] Cara Wicks-Ortega, a kindergarten teacher, says that, "some of these children have never been read to at home. Some have barely been talked to." She says, "I'm the teacher, substitute mother, counselor, nurse, and one-woman social welfare department."[19]

Learning Violence

Children learn aggressive behavior by watching others use violence and then imitating what they have seen. This process is called "modeling." Boys growing up surrounded by violent male role models may never see an adult man restrain his anger or control his impulses. Such children may never experience nonviolent discipline or see an adult resolve a dispute without violence.[20] Children who are abused or who see their mother being abused begin to see violence as a natural part of life. Studies have indicated that a boy whose father is a criminal is more likely to become a criminal himself, especially if the father is abusive or neglectful. Parents who encourage their children to solve problems with physical aggression and exhibit violent behavior themselves often produce children who are aggressive and violent.

Teenage friends who model violent behavior are an even more powerful influence on young people than adult models.[21] In some neighborhoods, violence is taken for granted and status may be based on fighting skills and a reputation for aggressive behavior. Children who grow up in such neighborhoods are at a high risk for displaying violent behavior.

Dan Shearer, a counselor and peer mediation coordinator at McClintock Middle School in Charlotte, North Carolina, says that, "Students are not violent at school because they are poor and exposed to drugs and crime. Students become violent because they have learned conflict as their primary means of interaction, and violence is a frequent outcome of conflict." These children, says Shearer, thrive on conflict. "Many of these students

21

measure their self-worth not on academic success, but on their performance in the conflict arena," he says. These children have been taught that a challenge must be met by a counter-challenge. They place a high value on being able to defend themselves verbally and physically. Shearer calls this "learned defensiveness" and says that any threat is responded to with a logical progression: defend, argue, confront, and attack. Shearer says that early intervention programs are needed to educate parents. He adds that schools must reinforce the fact that aggression is not an appropriate response to verbal conflict.[22]

Researchers studying the psychological effects of violence on young people found that witnessing violence at school was common. Approximately three out of four students reported seeing someone being threatened, slapped, hit, or punched at school during the past year. Of inner-city students, approximately half reported witnessing at least one shooting during the past year, and one third of the inner-city boys reported being shot at or shot during the past year.[23] The researchers compared exposure to violence with symptoms of psychological trauma such as anxiety, depression, post-traumatic stress, dissociation, and anger. Mark I. Singer, Ph.D., principal investigator for the study, says that "every measure was strongly associated with exposure to violence . . . as exposure went up, so did youth psychological trauma."[24] Singer and his colleagues also found that exposure to violence increased the likelihood that a student would exhibit violent behavior.

A growing number of children are failing at home, failing at school, and beginning to think that they will fail in life. As a result, they sink deeper and deeper into a well of hopelessness. Stephen Harper, Chief Juvenile Public Defender in Dade County, Florida, says:

> The fourteen-year-old kid who grows up in a community where even going to the corner store is a hostile experience and a threatening experience, and comes from a dysfunctional home, and has a lousy opportunity in school . . . he doesn't know he has a future, or worse, he knows he has none.[25]

These are the young people who may look for illegal ways to succeed or turn to gangs for the security, acceptance, and power that is missing in their lives.

Violence in the Media

Many school officials feel that the media play a major role in the increase in youth violence. Television programs, movies, and even music lyrics are often filled with violent images, violent heroes, and violent acts. Some feel that this has led to an increasing acceptance of violence as a way to solve problems.[26]

Children see violence in movies and on TV with no ethical context. It is exciting, satisfying, and empowering. Heroes live; villains die. No one ends up in a wheelchair without bowel control or in a hospital bed breathing through a tube.[27] In her book, *Deadly Consequences*, Deborah Prothrow-Stith says that television violence (violence without consequences) reinforces the magical way many children think. The young people who are shooting each other, says Prothrow-Stith, may not fully realize that death is permanent, unalterable, final, and tragic.[28] Judge Larabee has had two cases in which kids who had been playing video games went out and murdered someone, and then went back to playing video games. "There is no difference for them between 'Mortal Combat' and real life," she says.[29]

The Resolving Conflict Creatively Program (RCCP), a joint venture of the New York City Board of Education, Educators for Social Responsibility, and seven school districts, is attempting to change children's perceptions of violence. The teaching guide points out that children are exposed to vivid images of war and violence and see peace as the absence of excitement. One goal of the program is to erase the sissy image of nonviolence.[30]

Peg Phillips, the actress who played Ruth Ann on the television show "Northern Exposure," refuses to appear in television programs or movies that are overly violent. "I think the violence level on television is completely unacceptable," says Phillips, "and it simply can't help rubbing off on the viewers." For seven years, Phillips has led a creative acting class for serious offenders, aged ten to eighteen, in a locked facility in the Pacific Northwest. "Our kids . . . have been so exposed to and inured to violence that they hardly know anything else exists," Phillips says. She feels that drama gives the children an enjoyable way to escape their difficult lives and to learn about cooperation, relationships, and self-esteem. At the end of the year, the class puts on a production that is based on the kids' hopes and dreams. No violent themes are allowed.[31]

Heavy metal and rap music lyrics are also often violent. In-your-face lyrics mock authority and glorify guns. Women are often portrayed as victims of violence, or as deserving punishment. Some of the singers emphasize the violent nature of their music through their attire

Peg Phillips, who played Ruth Ann on "Northern Exposure," actively campaigns against violence in the media.

and appearance, what they say in interviews, and the way they behave in their personal lives. These messages add fuel to the anger of disillusioned young people.

Karl V. Hertz, superintendent of the Mequon-Thiensville school district in Mequon, Wisconsin, says that our society has accepted a new level of violence—in sports, movies, music videos, news broadcasts, books, and in our communities. This acceptance, says Hertz, sends the wrong signal to teenagers who are already struggling with anger and frustration. He says that athletes, entertainers, and others should take more responsibility for helping to reduce violence. Hertz feels that, "As Americans, we clearly have before us a goodness issue. We must attend to it."[32]

Young people admit that they listen to celebrities. When asked who would be the most effective spokesperson to help reduce and prevent student violence (the person they would be most likely to listen and pay attention to), 33 percent of students in grades three through twelve said a famous athlete; 20 percent chose a famous TV or movie actor.[33] So if young people would be affected by a celebrity's message promoting nonviolence, chances are they are being affected by celebrities who send messages promoting violence as well.

Substance Abuse

Illegal narcotic trafficking is big business in America, and one of the primary markets is school-age children. In a survey of students in grades nine through twelve, nearly one fourth of the students had been offered, sold, or given an illegal drug on school property during the thirty days preceding the survey.[34] Where there are drugs and drug dealing, there is violence.[35]

Crime rates are highest at schools where alcohol and illegal drugs are easily obtained.[36] Some illegal drugs are very strongly associated with displays of aggression and can trigger violent explosions.[37] Violence also results from drug dealers retaliating against other dealers, punishing unsatisfactory "employees," covering up illegal activities, and resisting school or law enforcement officials.

Although drug use among students has dropped somewhat, alcohol use has not. School-age drinkers consume 35 percent of the wine coolers and $1.5 billion worth of beer each year.[38] A study by the National Institute of Education found that over 3 million teenagers have alcohol problems. They discovered that one in four students in grades ten through twelve drank alcohol at least once a week, and that 6 percent of all twelfth-graders drank every day.[39] Significantly, alcohol appears to suppress inhibitions against violence in some people.[40]

Biology or Environment?

In every school there is at least one student who is known as a troublemaker. Are some kids just born bad? Could there be a "violent gene" or some other biological factor that determines who will achieve and who will get into trouble?

James Q. Wilson, professor of public policy at University of California, Los Angeles, says that 5 to 6 percent of young boys commit half or more of all serious crimes. This percentage holds true for every culture, according to Wilson. He lists the characteristics that young frequent offenders tend to share, which include: having a low verbal intelligence quotient (IQ) and doing poorly in school, not having many friends, having a criminal for a parent, experimenting with drugs at an early age, being impulsive, and having difficulty understanding other people's feelings.[41]

Recent research has examined the connection between criminal behavior and lower than average IQ. The incidence of mental retardation has been estimated at up to 30 percent of all criminal offenders.[42] The average IQ of convicted criminals is ninety-two, ten points lower than the average for law-abiding citizens.[43] IQ scores are particularly low among repeat offenders. Terrie E. Moffitt, a psychologist at the University of Wisconsin-Madison, has said that "Our results also suggest that poor verbal ability is the 'active ingredient' for delinquency in the [overall] IQ."[44] In contrast, young people who have been raised by abusive, neglectful parents or who live in high-crime areas, but nevertheless do not become criminals have higher than average IQs.

Another indicator researchers have found is that children who show fearless or impulsive behavior in their early years, often become aggressive and violent later.[45] Are impulsiveness and intelligence determined by genetics or by the child's environment? Some researchers feel that children who are impulsive and have low IQs may enter a downward spiral of poor relationships and other failures that leads to a life of criminal activity.[46]

Frederick Goodwin, M.D., former director of the National Institute of Mental Health, says that most violence is caused by a small proportion of young men who are repeatedly violent. As children, these men showed poor impulse control and excessive aggression, but only a small number of children with such behaviors (which affect all races and classes equally, according to Goodwin) grow up to be violent offenders. What shifts the odds, says Goodwin, are environmental factors such as poor living conditions and the absence of a father. Goodwin feels that psychological treatment and perhaps even medication for at-risk children could prevent later violence.[47]

Learning disabilities and other conditions may also play a part in violent behavior. It has been estimated that 40 percent of the United States prison population have a learning disability.[48] Attention Deficit Disorder with Hyperactivity during the teenage years can also be a predisposing factor in the development of problems such as vandalism, theft, substance abuse, assaults, and other crimes.[49]

Could violent crime have a biological basis, as alcoholism does? Some kinds of brain activity, the action of some chemicals, and the release of certain hormones can trigger violent outbursts. Severe head injury can also cause violent behavior.[50] Some researchers have suggested that abnormal levels of serotonin and noradrenaline might be to blame for some violent behavior. There may even be a genetic defect that causes the brain to produce excess quantities of these chemicals.[51] Social critic Robert Wright said in an article in *The New Yorker* that low serotonin levels may make people more prone to violence, and poor social conditions seem to lower serotonin levels.[52]

In nature, many male animals exhibit aggressive tendencies. Are male humans just naturally violent? Perhaps one day doctors will have a pill or an operation that prevents violent behavior. Who would decide who gets the "treatment"? Could the government or an agency force someone to take it?

Violence probably results from a combination of factors. Researchers from the APA have pointed to biological factors, such as heredity and head injury, as well as environmental factors, such as poor parenting, problems relating to peers, lack of opportunity, media influences, and poverty, as underlying causes of violent behavior.[53]

Violence is normal in the world of today's adolescent. . . . From Rambo to the corporate raiders, it's the aggressive, tough-minded guys who get the job done regardless of laws and the societal constraints. . . . They're the admirable, effective people.

—East Harlem principal, whose student was accused of taking part in the attack and rape of a jogger in New York's Central Park[1]

3

Guns and Gangs

Eighth-grade student John Sirola was sent to the principal's office at Sacred Heart School in Redlands, California. He had been having difficulties with the dress code and other rules at the Catholic school. After meeting with the principal, John left. He returned with a sawed-off shotgun and shot the principal in the face and shoulder. Then John walked out of school, shot himself in the chest, and died. A spokesman for the Roman Catholic Diocese of Riverside and San Bernardino counties explained the incident by saying: "He was simply a young man having a real tough time growing up." A fellow student added, "I think he kind of kept stuff inside of him."[2]

Young people have always had a tough time growing up, and it can be tougher for some than for others. What has changed is that the availability of guns makes it possible for a troubled student to instantly make an irrevocable decision, to administer a permanent solution to a temporary problem, and to make a mistake that ends a life or changes it forever.

A Gun Culture

The statistics are staggering. More American young people have been killed by guns in the last thirteen years than were killed during the entire Vietnam War. Every year since 1950, the number of American children killed with guns has doubled. Every two days, the equivalent of an entire classroom of kids (twenty-five) are killed by guns. Every three hours, someone between the ages of ten and nineteen is killed with a gun.[3]

Children no longer learn about guns from TV cowboys; they see them first-hand. In 1992, the Gun Safety Institute surveyed 450 fifth, seventh, and ninth graders in the Cleveland Public School system. The results showed that 87 percent of the students knew someone who had a gun, 52 percent had held a gun themselves, 11 percent owned a gun, 41 percent had seen someone shot, and 5 percent had been shot themselves.[4] According to a Baltimore City Grand Jury report, 60 percent of the Baltimore City Public School students surveyed knew someone who had been shot, threatened, or robbed in their school in a six-month period.[5] Exposure to gun violence is markedly higher in inner-city schools. One study found that one in four boys at two inner-city schools in Cleveland reported being shot at or shot, while less than 3 percent of boys at a suburban school in Cleveland reported being shot at or shot.[6]

America is a gun-loving culture. There are more than 211 million firearms in the possession of private citizens in the United States.[7] Guns and other weapons are not just in the home; they are in the streets and the schools. Nationwide, more than one in ten students say they carried a weapon on school property during the past thirty days.[8] Access to guns was named as a cause of violence by 43 percent of the school officials responding in a national survey.[9]

Gun-related incidents affect all kinds of students. Most offenders are male (93 percent), but so are most victims (76 percent). Of school incidents involving guns, 63 percent involved high school students, 24 percent junior high school students, 12 percent elementary students, and one percent preschoolers.[10] Gun-related incidents are most commonly sparked by gang or drug disputes (18 percent), long-standing arguments (15 percent), romantic disagreements (12 percent), or fights over material possessions (10 percent).[11]

Many students who carry guns say that they do so to protect themselves. George E. Butterfield, deputy director of the National School Safety Center, explains, "Students who would never be classified as troublemakers are arming themselves with knives, box cutters, and even guns because they don't feel safe in school."[12] Some students have to walk to school through a battlefield of drugs, violence, and crime. Allan Parachini, a public affairs director for the Los Angeles chapter of the American Civil Liberties Union who met with students to discuss school safety, commented that, "the students told us they weren't concerned about their safety in school. They were concerned about their safety going to

33

Keeping drugs out of schools is one way to reduce school violence.

or coming from school."[13] About one hundred sixty thousand students stay home each day because they are afraid of guns and violence.[14]

Students who do not carry weapons are hesitant to report those who do. A 1994 survey of students in grades seven through twelve found that only one in five would definitely tell a teacher if he or she knew a student had carried a weapon to school. The top reason for not reporting a weapon was fear of retaliation.[15]

In response to concerns about guns in and around schools, Congress enacted the Gun-Free School Zones Act of 1990. The act made it a federal crime to possess a firearm within a thousand feet of a school. In 1995, the Supreme Court overturned the law, ruling that Congress had exceeded its authority. The decision resulted from the appeal of a 1992 case in which a twelfth-grader was charged with carrying a concealed handgun to his San Antonio, Texas, high school. He said he was to be paid forty dollars for the gun, which was for use in a "gang war."

Most states have laws that outlaw guns on or near school grounds. These laws were unaffected by the Court ruling, but many school officials remain concerned. Bob Chase, vice president of the National Education Association, said, "We are dismayed that it is no longer illegal to carry a handgun in or near schools in some states."[16]

Gun Safety and Prevention

At one time, a disagreement between students might lead to a shove, a punch, or perhaps a fight. Today, a disagreement can end in death. The difference is the availability of guns. So, how do schools prevent students from bringing guns to school without making schools into prisons?

One solution is to develop guns that are childproof or that can only be fired by the owner, says Stephen Teret, director of the Johns Hopkins Center for Gun Policy and Research. Such guns might at least help prevent accidental injuries and deaths.[17] However, only 13 percent of the incidents involving gun violence are accidental.[18]

Why do teenagers carry guns? The Gun Safety Institute has identified four attitudes that contribute to gun use by young people. First, young people think that guns and people who carry them are exciting. Second, they feel that guns provide safety and power. Third, they think that the response to shame or disrespect is aggression, and fourth, young people are comfortable with aggression. The institute created a program to directly address these attitudes. The program, called "Solutions Without Guns," helps students identify attitudes in themselves that might lead to gun use and teaches them to choose more positive behaviors. It also helps students resist negative peer pressure and practice appropriate behaviors, while encouraging others to behave properly.[19]

Dealing with this problem involves not only trying to prevent guns from being brought to school, but trying to defuse potentially dangerous situations early. To accomplish this, students and teachers must be taught how to deal with hostile situations. In addition, schools should have firm policies on guns and other weapons, establish an emergency plan for the school, prevent drug activity on school grounds, and address the students' need for self-esteem—a need that can be met by carrying a symbol of power such as a gun.[20]

Education plays a big role in preventing gun violence. At West Charlotte High School, SAVE members conduct classes that teach students that a gun at school threatens everyone—including the student who carries it. Advisor Gary Weart warns students that even a gun inside a book bag can be deadly. ". . . you accidently slam your book bag to the ground, and it discharges, and you just shot and killed your best friend," Weart tells the students. He explains why weapons have no place in school. "If everybody is worried and everybody is tense, then we're wasting our time because learning can't take place if you're worried about somebody walking in that door and blowing somebody away."

Weart's message seems to have gotten through. "The year before we started SAVE," says Weart, "we had nine handguns. The year that we started SAVE [1989], we had two. . . . Since 1989, we've had one handgun, and that was brought to school by a janitor, to sell to another janitor, and they were turned in by a kid."[21]

Gangs

A gang is a group of people, usually of the same ethnic group and from the same neighborhood, who band together. They often take part in illegal activities and rebel against the rest of society. Many have certain areas or "turf" that they protect as their own territory. Although most gangs are made up of young men, female gangs are becoming more common. Even though many people think of black teenagers when they think of gangs, there are white, Asian, Hispanic, and even Samoan gangs.

For some young people, gangs provide the only emotional and physical security they have ever known. Gang membership can provide respect, power, family, and protection. Unfortunately, gang membership can also be very dangerous. Many gangs are not social or ethnic clubs, but crime organizations that may control area drug markets or extortion operations. Male gang members commit six times more crimes than non-gang members.[22]

Factors that motivate young people to join gangs include poor home situations (lack of supervision, drug use by parents, emotional isolation) and poor community environment (low community spirit, deteriorated buildings, few community resources). In addition, gangs are appealing to naturally rebellious teenagers, particularly those who have a weak self-image, few goals, and who fear physical harm.[23] Gangs also seem exciting and appeal to risk-taking teenagers. Some experts have gone so far as to say that gangs attract teenagers who enjoy crime and violence.[24]

Gang members maintain intense loyalty to the gang. "Being down" means doing anything for the gang, even if it means losing one's life or taking someone else's. Gang leaders often expect members to value each other above their own family members. In exchange, gang members receive pride, respect, and recognition from their peers. They are often feared by others and gain a sense of power in an otherwise powerless environment of poverty and hopelessness.[25]

Breaking away from a gang can be difficult, if not impossible, for some young people. Some gangs do not allow members to leave, and some gang members do not know any other life. In some areas, it is not so much a gang as a neighborhood. You are where you live.

Heather Thompson describes one girl's case:

> She had joined the BGDs (Black Gangster Disciples). It's one of the oldest gangs in Seattle. . . . When she was 12 she had been jumped in. And from that point on, she ran with the gangs in Seattle. . . . She had been shackled and gang-raped after being kidnapped from her house. . . . She had a friend of hers murdered and he died in her arms. All these types of things and she wasn't even 16. . . . She joined SAVE because she wanted to speak out and tell people what was going on. And then after a couple of meetings she left me a note that said that she couldn't participate in SAVE anymore because she joined another gang.[26]

Some teachers have sucessfully made peace with gang members, even though they hate the gangs themselves. S. B. Hawk, a teacher at James Monroe High School in Los Angeles Unified School District, teaches a remedial class for students who have failed required courses. "On a given day," she says, "there's 14 gangs sitting in here." Having rival gang members sit peacefully in the same room is a remarkable achievement. Her secret? She refused to let them push her around. "It was that simple. And for some reason, that's what they respected."

Hawk earned the gang members' trust. Before she got involved, gang members were blamed for everything. Hawk showed them that she believed in them. "I will send them to jail if they break the law," she says, "but I also will back them when they're accused of something they didn't do and I will do it right out in front of everybody and I'll go to the principal if I have to." From the beginning, she told them, "you don't lie to me and you don't con me. And you follow the rules or I get you locked up." When they have a dispute, they leave it outside. Those who cannot follow the rules are transferred out, which to many means jail.

Hawk is fifty-six, white, and does not speak a word of Spanish, even though she teaches at a school with three thousand students, more than half of whom are Hispanic. "I refer to myself as 'this old white woman that don't know a damn thing you're saying,'" she chuckles. Nevertheless, they know how she feels about violence. She tells them, "I will hire the bus. I'll send you all out to the desert and let you blow each other away. Leave the rest of us alone."

Her tough approach, combined with a solid conflict resolution program, has been an outstanding success. The school also prohibits clothing that carries gang identification, such as belt buckles. "I just have bags full of belt buckles that I take away from them," she laughs. "If they do come in and the pants are too big, I take the belt away from them and they have to walk around all day holding their pants up because I won't give them a pin."

Hawk's students know what is expected of them. They no longer carry weapons, the grafitti is gone, and problems are promptly reported. "They're the straightest students in school," says Hawk. "They're a good bunch of kids. Do they still do evil things? Yes. I wish I could say they didn't. But, man, they are graduating from high school. I mean, they're getting their diplomas. I am so proud of them I can't stand it."[27]

Carlos, eighteen, has been a member of the West Side Drifters in Los Angeles for ten years. Monroe High School was his last chance, "Cause I got kicked out of all the other schools for car jacking and all that stuff, you know, jacking stereos from the parking lot," he explains. "They gave me one more chance and I looked at everything that I had done and this was my last opportunity to change. . . . I thought to myself and I said 'I've been through too much, too many things, you know, for me to just throw it away' and so I just decided to do better." Now he's getting his diploma. "Before I was always, like, I really didn't care about school and stuff. Most of my home boys dropped out. They're all drop-outs. I'm going to be the first person in my family to graduate from high school."[28]

Gangs continue to be a major problem in many schools. Experts say there is no simple solution, but by working together, parents, community leaders, police officers, school officials, and teachers like Ms. Hawk can make a difference.

I'm always getting shot at and it sucks.

—an adolescent tired of violence[1]

4

Student-Against-Student Violence

Student-against-student violence can range from bullying other students to robbing, raping, or even killing them. There may be a single perpetrator or there may be dozens, and even though boys are the most common culprits, girls commit violent acts as well. The violence may be random or it may be targeted. Why do students hurt each other? What can be done to bring students together so that schools can be safer for everyone?

Bullying and Intimidation

Bullying. It is a familiar story: one kid picking on another for being chubby, wearing glasses, or talking funny. This may sound typical, but researchers say it is not accurate. Although victims of bullying may be younger and weaker than their tormentors, they are not necessarily students who are just different. Bullying has been defined as physical or psychological abuse toward individuals who are not able to defend themselves.[2] It is widespread. In a study of fourth through eighth graders in four midwestern schools, 90 percent reported being bullied.[3] The most likely victims of bullying are people who are anxious, insecure, cautious, sensitive, and quiet. These individuals have poor opinions of themselves and feel stupid, ashamed, or unattractive. They usually are not aggressive and may be physically weaker than other students. When attacked, they cry or withdraw. In short, they are easy marks for the bullies who torment them.

Researchers have found no evidence that bullies act the way they do because they are insecure. What researchers have found is that bullies tend to be aggressive, have a positive attitude toward violence, are impulsive, and have a strong need to dominate others. Some come from family situations in which they have developed hostility, perhaps even a sense of satisfaction from hurting someone else. They may use their bullying to get cigarettes, money, or other items of value, or they may do it to get respect from friends. Four factors seem to contribute to the development of bullying behavior: a negative attitude toward the child by the parent or caretaker, a permissive and tolerant attitude toward the child's aggressive behavior, a parenting style that uses power and violence to control the child, and a natural tendency for the child to be hot-headed.[4]

Most bullies are boys, but girls can be bullies as well. Girl bullies often use indirect methods, such as spreading rumors, manipulating friends, lying about other students, and excluding others from the group. Researchers have also discovered a phenomenon called "passive bullies." These are the students who stand on the sidelines, encouraging bullies and perhaps even taking part, but do not start the bullying on their own.[5]

Why are researchers interested in learning about bullies? Studies have shown that approximately 60 percent of boys who were bullies in sixth through ninth grades were convicted of at least one crime by age twenty-four. As many as 35 to 40 percent had three or more convictions. Only 10 percent of a comparable group of nonbullies had records of this type. Former victims of bullies also suffered lasting effects. They were more likely to be depressed and have poor self-esteem.[6]

Researchers say bullying can be reduced if schools take an active role. By establishing and enforcing rules against bullying, providing support and protection for the victims, increasing awareness of the problem, and involving teachers and parents, schools can limit bullying behavior.

Black-on-Black Violence

The world that surrounds many inner-city African-American adolescents is a world of unemployment, poverty, overcrowded and unhealthy living conditions, poor education and job-training, inadequate healthcare, criminally inclined peer groups, and a segregated existence. In his book *Understanding Black Adolescent Male Violence: Its Remediation and Prevention*, Amos N. Wilson says that these problems are compounded by the breakdown of the family and a period of conservative, if not hostile, government. The urban world has been flooded with addictive drugs, infectious diseases, and guns, says Wilson. This world provides few opportunities for African-American men to achieve success through manufacturing, retailing, service, or professional activity. Wilson contrasts this reality with the messages these adolescents receive from the outside world. Television, mass marketing, and advertising create artificial needs and high expectations, yet African-American adolescents have limited means of fulfilling them. This leads to tremendous frustration and anger.[7]

Psychologist Louis Ramey suggests that African-American males living in poverty are awash in what he calls "free-floating anger," a feeling that the deck is stacked against them. Any small provocation can ignite the volatile feelings of frustration, helplessness, and anger that they carry with them. They strike out at the nearest target, which is often another African-American adolescent.[8]

Another theory that attempts to explain black-on-black violence is that of black self-hatred. According to this theory, racism has taught poor African-American males to hate themselves. Because of this, they assault and murder people who resemble them.[9]

Wilson blames white racism for black-on-black violence. He says that the aftereffects of racism may include chronic anger and frustration, displaced aggression, internalization of racist attitudes, and feelings of vulnerability, powerlessness, and hopelessness. Wilson feels that social scientists have failed to examine black-on-black violence in the context of white-on-black violence and white criminality in general. This, says Wilson, has led to a

46

Some people feel that television has contributed to violence in the streets and violence in the schools.

misinterpretation of the causes of black-on-black violence and has resulted in the stereotyping of blacks, especially young black males, as innately criminal.[10]

Racial, Ethnic, and Cultural Differences

Sometimes school violence stems not from a disagreement between students or from unfocused anger, but from hatred. Hatred not of what someone does but of what someone is. These incidents are sometimes referred to as "hate crimes" because they stem from an individual's or group's hatred of an entire race, ethnic group, or other classification. According to one survey, 28 percent of school violence is of a racial or ethnic nature.[11]

The United States has become such a melting pot of cultures that few classrooms contain students who all share the same background. In most classes, there are one or more students from a minority group—a racial, religious, cultural, or ethnic group that is represented in smaller numbers than the majority group. In 1990, minority students made up more than 50 percent of the school populations in California, Arizona, New Mexico, and Texas.[12] Some school districts have students from over a hundred different countries.

Whether you are considered a minority depends on where you live. In many inner-city schools, white students are in the minority, and in many suburban areas, black students are in the minority. Other areas may have Asian, Native American, Hispanic, or Pacific Islander minority groups. The smaller the size of a minority group in the school, the larger the chance that members of that group will be victimized by members of other groups.[13] Studies also show that the greater the physical differences between two groups, the higher the incidence of prejudice.[14]

Violence that results from racial or ethnic conflicts often takes time to develop. As early as 1958, social scientists identified a progression that characterizes such conflicts. First, people communicate their prejudicial attitudes to those who share their views. (This might take the form of demeaning jokes, misinformation about racial or ethnic characteristics, or fears regarding the group's activities or motivations.) Second, they break contact with the other ethnic or racial group. (This establishes "turf" and cuts off the lines of communication.) Third, they exclude the other ethnic or racial group from certain social functions. Fourth, they may physically attack a member of the other group. Fifth, they seek to actually exterminate the other group.[15]

Sometimes, hate violence takes the form of vandalism or indirect threats. For example, vandals may deface a Black History Month display, trash the lockers of certain students, or paint ethnic slurs on buildings. While the cost of the property damage may be low, these types of incidents can fuel tensions, increase hostility, and lead to more serious violence.

Prejudice is often the result of lack of experience with members of another group. In diverse communities, people grow up knowing members of other groups as individuals, not as faceless stereotypes. Racially mixed communities actually have the lowest levels of racial prejudice. Communities that are predominantly one race

49

have the most prejudice and the highest levels of racial violence.[16]

Sometimes conflicts can result, not from differences in appearance, but from differences in language or culture. Body language, subtle verbal cues, and even facial expressions can trigger unexpected responses in people from other backgrounds. For example, children from the Appalachian mountain area are brought up to believe so strongly that cowardice is bad that they will allow themselves to be punished, even if they are innocent, rather than risk having others think they are afraid of the punishment. However, they also feel that unjust punishment must be avenged, so a child who has been wrongly punished may later set a fire or retaliate in some other way.[17]

Cultural codes can bind people to certain courses of action. In some cultures, an insult requires a response. An accidental bump in a hallway may be interpreted as a challenge that must be answered. Touching may be viewed as an aggressive act, a violation of one's personal space, rather than a sign of affection. Direct eye contact can be seen as a challenge.

Poor male adolescents often place a great deal of emphasis on respect. As a result, they may find it impossible to walk away when they feel someone has insulted them. Yet as much as they want respect, they may have trouble showing respect for others because they feel it makes them look powerless. This can lead to confrontations and violence.[18]

To prevent racial, ethnic, and cultural conflicts, schools should encourage better interaction through education, communication, and conflict resolution. They can also make it clear that racist remarks and intimidation will not be tolerated. The earlier preventive techniques are started the better. Ideally, children should learn to understand and tolerate racial, ethnic, and cultural differences from an early age.

Gay Bashing

"Faggot!" "Dyke!" "Fruit Loop!" If you are smiling at these terms, chances are you have not experienced the pain of being singled out and tormented, threatened, perhaps even attacked by other students, for something you feel you cannot change. According to the Federal Bureau of Investigation, 46 percent of hate crimes that involve injury are based on sexual orientation (compared to 41 percent for race).[19]

Our society's prejudice against homosexuality has spilled over into the schools, where young people are super-sensitive to fitting in, gaining acceptance, and being "normal." The result is a climate of fear. When public school students in grades eight through eleven were asked to rate how upset they would be if they were the target of fourteen different types of sexual harassment, 85 percent of the boys put being called gay at the top of their lists. No other type of harassment, including actual physical abuse, was as feared. In the same survey, 23 percent of boys and 10 percent of girls reported having been called gay.[20]

Accurate statistics regarding antigay violence in schools are hard to come by, given the reluctance of many students to mention their sexual orientation in reporting an incident at school. A survey conducted by the National School Boards Association stated that 3 percent

51

Even the youngest children can be taught how to prevent violence.

of school violence is against gay and lesbian youths.[21] However, this estimate seems impossibly low since most crime reports show that a large number of gay men and lesbians are the victims of violence. In addition, almost 29 percent of offenders in antigay incidents are under the age of eighteen.[22] This means that a large number of perpetrators are of school age. A study by the National Gay and Lesbian Task Force found that nearly half of gay males and one fifth of lesbian females were harassed, threatened, or physically assaulted in high school because they were perceived to be homosexual.[23]

Almost 40 percent of antigay attacks are by two or more offenders.[24] Male adolescents may be responding to an inner conflict over their own sexuality and have a strong need to prove to their peers that they are not gay. In addition, some gay and lesbian teens go through a period of gay-bashing on their way to coming to terms with their own orientation. One teen referred to herself as "the gay-basher from hell" when she looked back at her own actions.[25]

Antigay violence can be physical or it can be psychological. Either way, it leaves lasting marks. Donald was harassed continuously in high school. "The guy behind me would reach up and tap me on the shoulder and say 'Hey, have you ever been with a girl? You ever did this or that?' and start giggling and making jokes. And the whole time, I'm trying to sit there and watch what's going on and I've got people around me giggling and laughing at me and making fun of me for being gay."

Like many gay teens who are harassed, Donald withdrew. As a result, his life changed direction. "The only thing I found that worked [in dealing with the intimidation] was staying at home," says Donald. "On the weekends, I didn't go out. I didn't socialize. I made myself a singular member of society, I guess. . . . I started drinking. I started smoking pot. I started going downhill. I quit school. . . . I was isolated completely."[26]

Isolation is an almost universal experience of gay and lesbian youth. The result, in some cases, is suicide. One study found that 20 percent of the white gay males and 25 percent of the white lesbians in the sample had actually attempted suicide. Other gay teens, rejected by family and friends, end up on the streets, where high-risk behavior such as prostitution and drug use can become a form of slow suicide.[27] According to a report issued by the U.S. Department of Health and Human Services in 1989, suicide is the leading cause of death for gay, lesbian, bisexual, and transsexual youth.[28]

Donald, who is now HIV-positive, says:

> Looking back, I feel like to me that was a form of suicide. Because my friends say they tried suicide and they thought about it. I never thought about it. I always told myself I was strong. I was stronger than that. Actually, I feel like I was so weak, I never had the nerve to say "I'm going to kill myself and get it over with." What I did was behavior that was detrimental to my health, to my body, to my life. . . . There were only a few things to live for. That was myself, that was drinking, doing drugs, spending money, and finding a boyfriend. Those were the things that were important to me. Now it's changed. Drastically.[29]

Tamara, who is now twenty, says that students at her high school yelled "faggot" and other names at her in the hallways, even though she had never told anyone of her orientation. "I felt threatened," she says, "like somebody was invading my territory." At one point, she was concerned enough that she began to carry a pocketknife to school. Then she decided to take the power away from her tormenters. She showed up at school wearing a shirt that read, "Nobody knows I'm a lesbian."

"I just wanted to put everybody's little mind at ease," she recalls, "and say 'this is me and if you can't deal with it then leave.'" She thinks that people were threatened by the fact that she felt confident enough to wear the shirt (even though she was shaking inside), so they left her alone.[30]

Gay and lesbian students face problems so severe that the New York City Board of Education, in conjunction with the Institute for the Protection of Lesbian and Gay Youth, created a separate school for them. The Harvey Milk School allows gay and lesbian students who are unable to attend a regular public school, due to fear of violence and harassment, to learn in a safe environment.

Both Tamara and Donald feel that teachers and administrators play a key role in setting guidelines for acceptable treatment of gay and lesbian students. When the school authorities take a stance that makes it clear that harassment and intimidation will not be tolerated, gay and lesbian students can feel more secure in school.

Dating Violence

Angela was sixteen when she began dating her brother's best friend, a guy she had practically grown up with. It was like a dream come true. Steve (not his real name) was eighteen, captain of the football team, and one of the most popular kids in their small town. Then one day Angela was in band class talking to two male friends when Steve came to pick her up. When they got to the car, he suddenly slapped her leg. Then he knocked her head into the windshield. He called her a "slut" and told her, "If I ever see you talking to them again, I'm going to hurt you worse." "I was just shocked," recalls Angela. "I didn't know what to do. I didn't know what to say. I just sat there. I really didn't understand at all what was going on and I thought maybe I did do something wrong that I shouldn't have done." Scared, ashamed, and confused, Angela continued the relationship for a year and a half, despite continuous abuse. "He used to tell me that I was fat and ugly and that nobody would ever want me and that I was lucky to have someone like him." She endured black eyes and bruised ribs, being knocked through a door and thrown down stairs. She became anorexic and considered suicide.

Like many abusers, Steve would say he was sorry. He would give Angela gifts and seem to feel bad about what he had done. Nevertheless, he kept up the abuse. Why did she stay with him? "I was just afraid that I would get hurt worse if I tried to leave," she says.

Eventually, Angela found the strength to break up with Steve. "He threatened to kill me and my family and anybody who was close to me," she says. But she decided, "either I'm going to die in this relationship or I'm going to die out of it. . . . I'd rather die out of it than in it." Steve continued to stalk her after they broke up but eventually he moved on. Still, Angela has had trouble getting her confidence back. "At first it was really difficult to get close to anybody," she says. "If my boyfriend got mad at me, it would really scare me." And she's still overly concerned about the way she looks. "My self esteem really isn't back to normal. . . . But I'm working on it."

Unfortunately, many teenagers have abusive relationships but never tell anyone. Bruises can be hidden and excuses given. "I think it's very common," says Angela, "but people just don't want to talk about it."[31]

Dating relationships that involve violence follow the same pattern as domestic violence between adult men and women. The man (usually) may restrict the woman's activities; show extreme jealousy; hit, punch, kick, or otherwise injure the woman; physically restrain her; force her to perform sex acts against her will; or verbally abuse her with threats or insults. The goal is to control the victim. Both partners may be violent, or only one, and alcohol or drug use is often involved. Breakups and reconciliations are common. The victims often blame themselves, and the abuser often denies there is a problem.

It is difficult to know how much school violence is related to dating violence. However, a report on gun violence attributed 12 percent of gun-related incidents to "romantic disagreements."[32]

Rape

Although most people think about rape as an adult woman being attacked by a stranger, rape occurs any time someone has sexual intercourse with another person without his or her consent. The victim is damaged emotionally as well as physically. Misconceptions about the crime of rape and the poor way in which law enforcement and the courts have handled rape in the past can compound the fear, guilt, embarrassment, and shame many rape victims feel.

Rape has nothing to do with physical attractiveness or temptation. Rape victims may be babies or grand-mothers. They may weigh eighty pounds or three hundred pounds. They may be wearing mini-skirts or their fathers' winter coats. They may not even be women. Men are victims in 10 percent of sexual assaults.[33] Rape is an act of violence perpetrated by a stranger, an acquaintance, a friend, or even a spouse.

Teenagers may be the victims or the perpetrators of rape. Most rape victims are between ten and nineteen years of age.[34] A survey of 105 convicted sex offenders in the state of Washington revealed that almost half of them had committed their first offense before age seventeen.[35] For this reason, teenagers need to be knowledgeable about this form of violence in order to protect themselves in and out of school. According to one survey, 7 percent of the violent acts committed in schools involved rape. In urban school districts, the number approached 20 percent.[36]

Many people think that rape is something that happens only in big cities, but no area is immune. In a survey of students at two schools located in the centers of large cities, one located in a small city, and one located in a suburban area, approximately one in six females reported having been forced to do an unwanted sexual act at least once in the last year. The rate of sexual abuse or assault of female students was actually higher at the small city school than at either inner-city school.[37] Heather Thompson found that affluent Redmond, Washington, had its share of sexual assaults as well. A friend she had grown up with was stalked and brutally raped by a boy-friend. Thompson later found out that other friends had been raped, yet none of them had ever reported it. "I can't name all the girls that I know that have been raped," she says. "But there are quite a few. What I *can* say is that it is in schools in the suburbs. You can't just say that it's not there. You can't assume it's not there because there's money where you live."[38]

One form of rape that people have become more conscious of recently is date rape. Date rape, or acquain-tance rape, refers to an act of nonconsensual sexual intercourse in which the victim knows the attacker or has gone out with him voluntarily. However, as in all forms of rape, the victim did not give his or her consent to have sex.

Angela had told Steve she did not want to have sex until marriage. He had said he respected her decision, but one day, after hitting her and throwing her up against a wall, Steve raped her. "He didn't really say any-thing," Angela recalls, "he just threw me on the bed and started taking my clothes off and everything. . . . I didn't want to do anything [to stop him] because I knew he'd probably hurt me worse." It was Angela's first sexual experience.

Like many rape victims, Angela felt guilty. "I felt really bad," she says. "I felt worse for my parents because they taught me so much—values and things like that. I thought I had disrespected them by what had gone on,

Heather Thompson speaks about violence in a SAVE presentation.

even though it wasn't my fault. I somehow thought it was . . . I was just really ashamed."[39]

In as many as 75 percent of date rape cases, alcohol or drugs are involved.[40] An impaired victim can misjudge a potentially dangerous situation, may be unconscious, or may not be able to fight off an attacker. An impaired attacker may be more violent, have fewer inhibitions, and be less inclined to consider the feelings and desires of the victim. Regardless of the circumstances, however, the responsibility always lies with the attacker. If the victim is unable to give consent or has said "no," it's not sex, it's rape.

Sexual Harassment

Sexual harassment is a problem that is often overlooked in schools. It can include any of the following: sexual comments, inappropriate touching, staring or leering, offensive noises, displays of sex-related objects or materials, obscene gestures or jokes, sexual gossip or suggestions, pressure for sexual activity, blocking a person's movement, flashing or mooning, spying on people while they are changing clothes or showering, and pulling or lifting clothing. Sometimes confused with flirting, sexual harassment is not mutual. While one person is having a good time, the other is not. In fact, the victim may feel intimidated, frightened, and powerless. And although perpetrators may say it is "all in good fun," it is the feeling of control that many of them enjoy.

In 1993, the American Association of University Women (AAUW) commissioned Louis Harris and Associates to conduct the first major United States study of sexual harassment in schools. The survey of sixteen hundred public school students in grades eight through eleven found that four out of five students experienced unwanted and unwelcome sexual behavior either at school or during a school-related activity. Almost a third reported first experiencing harassment during grades six through nine.[41]

Sexual harassment is not harmless fun; it can affect the student's ability to learn. Students who have been harassed tend to stay home, cut classes, not speak up in class, and make lower grades more often than students who have not been victimized. The AAUW survey found that over 30 percent of the girls and over 10 percent of the boys who had been sexually harassed reported not wanting to go to school as a result.[42]

The AAUW survey found that incidents of sexual harassment often took place in hallways or classrooms, raising the question of how adult supervision failed to protect victims. The survey, which has been termed a "wake-up call" for educators and school administrators, may help increase understanding and improve prevention of this problem. Measures that can help prevent sexual harassment include providing good supervison, setting clear guidelines for acceptable behavior, eliminating potentially dangerous areas, educating students and teachers about sexual harassment, and counseling students who have been victims of sexual harassment.

Suicide

Suicide is a form of personal violence that affects not only the person who has taken his or her own life, but family and friends as well. In addition, one suicide can trigger other suicides, particularly among adolescents.

The teenage years are rough, even under the best of circumstances. For some teens, the loss of a boyfriend or girlfriend, failing grades, a ruined reputation, or other disappointments may seem insurmountable. Many young people have difficulty seeing that things can change and that the future holds many undiscovered opportunities. For these reasons, thoughts of suicide seem to haunt many adolescents. For some, a passing thought may turn to serious consideration. One study found that nearly one fourth of the students surveyed had seriously considered attempting suicide during the past year, and 8.6 percent had actually attempted suicide.[43]

Teen suicide has become an epidemic. From 1952 through 1992, the incidence of suicide among adolescents and young adults almost tripled. From 1980 to 1992, suicide rates among white youths between the ages of ten and fourteen rose 86 percent for males and 233 percent for females. Among black males, the suicide rate rose 164 percent among those between fifteen and nineteen years old, and 300 percent among those between ten and fourteen.[44]

Causes of suicide are complicated and often involve numerous factors. Some possible reasons for the increase in the number of suicides among certain groups include substance abuse, firearm availability, family violence, severe stress, and impulsive behavior. A variety of suicide prevention programs have been established and the reduction of the youth suicide rate is one of the national health objectives for the year 2000.

I was striking back at the educational system and it felt good. I could be just as tough and rough with them as they was with me.

—a young man expelled for vandalizing a school[1]

5

Other Violence in School

School violence is not always students hurting other students. Sometimes teachers, administrators, or other school employees are attacked by students, and sometimes students are the victims of violence perpetrated by school employees. Schools are vandalized, marred with graffiti, broken into, and burned down. School violence is a broad problem with far-reaching consequences that affect the entire school community.

Violence Against Teachers and Administrators

The National Center for Education Statistics announced in 1991 that nearly one in five school teachers reported being verbally abused by students, 8 percent reported being physically threatened, and 2 percent reported being attacked during the previous year.[2] During the

1992 to 1993 school year, 28 percent of all school districts surveyed experienced a student attack on a teacher. In urban areas, the number jumped to 60 percent.[3]

Verbal abuse of teachers has become more common. Nearly half of the school executives surveyed said that the incidence of "mouthing off" to teachers and administrators has increased.[4] Some cite the popularity of television programs that glamorize young actors who use put-downs, insults, and obscene gestures. Such behavior is presented in a way that makes it seem not only acceptable, but desirable. On television, disrespectful behavior is funny, effective, and rarely punished. In reality, it gets students in trouble, interferes with the learning process, affects the students' relationships with teachers and other students, and contributes to teacher burn-out.

Almost twenty years ago, counselors began seeing a cluster of symptoms they termed the "battered teacher syndrome." The combination of stress symptoms included anxiety, depression, sleeplessness, headaches, high blood pressure, and eating disorders.[5] Psychiatrist Alfred M. Bloch, M.D., studied inner-city school teachers who had sought psychiatric help. He compared them to war veterans who suffer from "combat neurosis." Like war veterans, the teachers saw guns, knives, and other weapons; witnessed violent acts; and in some cases, were physically attacked themselves. As a result, the teachers suffered from the same kinds of psychiatric symptoms as combat veterans.[6]

Some teachers deal with the stress of violence by becoming activists. Gary Weart, the advisor for SAVE at West Charlotte High School, has had twelve students murdered in twenty years of teaching. He now spends

Gary Weart turned his anger into action. He now spends much of his time helping to get out the SAVE message.

much of his time campaigning against violence. He still mourns the students he has lost but has turned his sadness and anger into action. "Every time it happens," he says, "it just empowers me not to attend another funeral."[7]

Arson, Vandalism, and Other Crimes Against Property

One of the most common forms of school violence is damage to school property, or vandalism. Although window-breaking is the most common type of vandalism, arson is the most costly, making up about 40 percent of total vandalism costs each year. From 1950 to 1975, the number of students attending public schools increased by 86 percent, but school arson increased 859 percent.[8]

Experts have found a number of factors that seem to contribute to vandalism. One is the simple enjoyment of destruction. Legendary child development expert Jean Piaget noted that destruction is a common type of play activity among children.[9] Just as toddlers enjoy smashing a stack of blocks, vandals enjoy breaking glass, knocking over desks, or other destructive activities. Vandals may also feel a sense of accomplishment, particularly if they are individuals who have had few opportunities to experience accomplishment in an acceptable way. Researchers have suggested that destruction is a simple and direct way for a person to have an impact on the world—to have control.

Vandalism may also give an individual a way to stand out from the crowd. By taking a risk and then succeeding, his or her social status may rise, and this acceptance by his or her peers rewards the vandal and improves his or her self-image. Vandalism is generally

68

not a crime that someone does alone and then does not tell anyone about. It is often a group of individuals who encourage one another and who also seek recognition from others by telling them about their actions.

Vandalism may result from the fact that the individuals involved want to leave their mark on the world. In years past, students carved their initials on desks as a way to go down in history. Graffiti may be the modern equivalent. In addition, schools are not "owned" by anyone and may seem like fair game to someone who would not damage a friend or neighbor's property. Writing graffiti or spray painting walls may be a way of declaring ownership. Gang members often use graffiti to declare turf, advertise gang activities, and recruit new members.

Sometimes student play becomes destructive, resulting in intentional or unintentional damage. Students who stuff towels in a toilet, for example, may be having fun, but the result can be costly repairs. Damage can also occur when other students egg someone on—encouraging him or her to do more than what the student meant to do. Experts say that schools need to do more to educate students about the limited funding schools receive and the need to protect school resources for everyone's benefit. By setting up a system that rewards those who economize, vandalism may be reduced.[10]

High schools that suffer the least vandalism are the smaller private schools and schools in small towns or communities where there is a family atmosphere and sense of security. What seems to protect a school from vandalism is the connection of the students to the school, the connection of the parents to the school, and community involvement. Large, complex schools in urban areas are often impersonal bureaucracies that have little connection with students and families. Additionally, they may be located in areas where members of the community may feel unconnected not only with the school, but with society. The anger and frustration of students and area residents may be expressed through acts of vandalism.[11]

Vandalism causes more than property damage. It damages the confidence of students, teachers, and staff members, and destroys the school community's peace of mind. It also interferes with the job of the school—education—by disrupting schedules, removing resources, and, in some cases, preventing teaching from taking place. It can create an atmosphere of fear and cause anxiety among students and staff. Vandalism can also hurt the school community's ability to work together, to trust, and to relate to each other.[12]

In responding to vandalism, school officials may react by flexing their power through police presence, surveillance, or other controlling techniques. Or they may use more subtle methods in an attempt to win the students and community over, portraying the school as a victim in need of help, involving the school in the community, and redefining the services the school provides. Or school officials may negotiate with students for their help in preserving the school, perhaps even giving them more power and responding to their complaints.[13]

Teacher-Student Violence

Often left out of discussions of school violence are acts committed by teachers against students. This can take the form of excessive corporal punishment, overreaction to a student attack, sexual harassment, or sexual abuse.

Although it is less common now than it was years ago, corporal punishment is still legal in some areas. In these places, teachers and school administrators are allowed to punish students physically. Usually there are specific guidelines as to what is considered acceptable, and permission from parents is often required. Nevertheless, physical punishment can be a form of violence when it is administered in areas where corporal punishment is not allowed or when guidelines are not followed.

Teachers who are attacked by students are within their rights to defend themselves. However, a teacher, like any individual, may lose control when verbally harassed or physically attacked. Overreaction can make a volatile situation even more dangerous.

Sexual harassment or abuse by teachers includes vulgar language, inappropriate touching, showing explicit pictures, and "affairs" between students and teachers. A survey of students in grades eight through eleven found that, of students who have reported sexual harassment, 18 percent named adults such as teachers, bus drivers, coaches, principals, or counselors as the perpetrators.[14]

A sexual relationship between an adult and a child, even if the child initiates it, is considered abusive. This is because adults have power over children and can use physical or psychological force to achieve their goals. Children, due to their inexperience and lack of knowledge, are not considered capable of giving their permission for sexual acts.

A sexual relationship does not have to involve a child to be considered abusive. Any time one individual holds

71

power over another, whether it is psychological power (psychiatrists or counselors), emotional or spiritual power (relatives or clergy), or the power to affect the individual's well-being (employers or school officials), sexual activity cannot be truly consensual. These kinds of power can be just as coercive as a rapist's knife or gun.

A teacher-student sexual relationship involves not only an abuse of the teacher's power but the abuse of an adult's power over a child. Even if a student feels he or she is entering into the relationship freely, the power the teacher holds over the student makes the relationship unequal and may make it difficult for the student to end the relationship without being penalized. Because force is involved, sexual harassment and abuse of students by teachers or other school employees can be considered a form of violence.

To deal with this type of violence, schools should maintain open lines of communication so that students feel safe reporting teacher-student violence. All incidents should be investigated and the proper authorities informed. Staff members and students should understand what is considered acceptable behavior and be alert to situations that could lead to abuse. In addition, school systems need to develop specific policies against such behaviors as inappropriate touching, giving gifts or special privileges to a particular student, attempting to hide interaction with a student, and having a peer rather than a professional relationship with a student.[15]

Poverty is the mother of crime.

—Marcus Aurelius, emperor of Rome, A.D. 161–180.[1]

6

Prevention and Treatment

Many kinds of programs have been developed in an attempt to address school violence. They include security measures, disciplinary actions, conflict resolution training, peer mediation programs, parent involvement, educational programs, sensitivity training, and support groups. Unfortunately, there is no magic answer. William Modzeleski, who coordinates antiviolence programs for the U.S. Department of Education, says, "There is no one program, no silver bullet, so that you can get one program up and say, 'Here it is—if you put this program in your school, you are going to resolve violence.' [The schools] are going to have to work with families and the communities."[2]

Student Rights vs. Public Safety
School officials must balance the school's need to maintain order against the students' right to privacy.

Organizations such as the North Carolina Center for the Prevention of School Violence are working to educate and involve the public.

Although students do not leave their constitutional rights at the door when they enter school, school officials have assumed broad authority in investigating incidents, searching students, and administering discipline.

School officials have more freedom to conduct searches than police officers. They do not need warrants or even "probable cause," the two conditions required by the Fourth Amendment. School officials have said that these requirements would seriously harm their ability to maintain discipline and create a safe school environment. Bernard James, special counsel for the National School Safety Center, says ". . . as the seriousness of the lawlessness increases, so too increases the flexibility of the school administrator in bringing to bear various enforcement solutions."[3]

The landmark case dealing with searches and student rights was *New Jersey* v. *T.L.O.* (1985). Before that time, it was questionable whether students were covered under the Fourth Amendment, which protects people from unlawful and unreasonable searches. The case dealt with a student (T.L.O.) who, with a friend, was found smoking cigarettes in a school bathroom by a teacher. The teacher took the students to the principal's office because they were in violation of a school rule. T.L.O. told the assistant vice principal that she had not been smoking and, in fact, did not smoke at all. The assistant vice principal demanded to see her purse. When he opened it, he found a pack of cigarettes and a package of rolling papers. On searching further, he found marijuana, a pipe, plastic bags, a lot of money, a list of students who owed T.L.O. money, and two letters that implicated her in marijuana dealing. T.L.O. wanted this evidence suppressed, but the Court upheld the search.

The T.L.O. case established a "two-prong" test: Those making the search must have a reasonable suspicion that the student has broken school rules or the law, and the search must be reasonable given the student's age and sex and the nature of the infraction. Cases after T.L.O. have maintained a common sense approach that requires school officials and security guards at schools to use good judgment and not search students or their belongings without "reasonable suspicion."[4]

Metal detectors are commonly used to screen all students as they enter the school. These "suspicionless" searches are more controversial. However, if there is reasonable suspicion that guns are entering the school, the school may be able to justify general searches. The trend is that random or blanket searches are acceptable, unless they are used to target certain ethnic groups or individuals.[5]

Physical Security

One way to prevent crimes from taking place in school is to design the school in a way that makes it difficult for the criminal to act without being observed, eliminates the criminal's access to victims and property, cuts off possible escape routes, assures rapid police intervention, and increases the chances that the criminal will be identified. Schools can also be built in ways that are less tempting to vandals. If something looks as if it would break in an interesting way, or looks as though it would be exciting to break, it may provoke vandalism.[6] Areas that are isolated or difficult to monitor, such as blind hallways, remote classrooms, or stairwells, can be redesigned or eliminated. Experts say that security should affect virtually every school activity. It should be a consideration in the planning and construction of schools, the scheduling of events, even the designing of landscaping.[7]

Violence caused by outsiders can be prevented by improving security procedures, fencing the school grounds, being alert to gang activities, listening for disputes that could lead to violence, and training teachers and students how to protect themselves and their belongings. In larger schools, identification tags are often used so that outsiders can be recognized.

Some experts feel that it is a mistake to concentrate too much on physical security and policing. They say that controlling behavior too tightly may prevent students from becoming independent thinkers and that too much emphasis on control fails to teach students how to prevent violence through mediation and other techniques.[8] In addition, physical security may change the students' perception of the school from a place of learning to a place of imprisonment. Others feel that the protection of the health and safety of all students demands that all methods of prevention be employed.

Search and Surveillance

Metal detectors have become a popular tool for fighting school violence. About 15 percent of all school districts have installed metal detectors, but in urban areas, the number rises to 39 percent.[9] Nevertheless, The Centers for Disease Control and Prevention say that metal detectors "have no apparent effect on the number of injuries, deaths, or threats of violence" in schools.[10]

Many teachers agree that metal detectors are not the solution. In a 1994 survey conducted by the Honeywell Corporation on how to control violence, 82 percent named training for parents, 78 percent mentioned smaller classes, 77 percent wanted stricter discipline, 76 percent called for schools to provide family support systems, and 72 percent pointed to more student involvement in disciplinary matters. Only 30 percent felt that metal detectors or security guards were the answer.[11] Tom Shriver, supervisor of the New Haven, Connecticut, school district's social development department, says metal detectors "cast a shadow over the quality, the potential, the competency, the youthful optimism that kids have. I think schools have to be places that promote the positive in children. Metal detectors give evidence of failure and weakness."[12] Gary Weart, advisor for SAVE, says, "My feeling on metal detectors is very, very strong. Metal detectors are reactive, short-term. If a kid's bringing a weapon to school . . . it's an indication of a deeper-seated problem. The weapon is the manifestation of the problem. It could be abuse, it could be drugs, it could be health care, it could be harassment, it could be whatever, but that's why that weapon is coming to school."[13]

Metal detectors have many limitations. Most schools can only spot-check because scanning every student would take too long. Also, kids can easily hide weapons under a heavy belt buckle or beat the system in other ways. The presence of metal detectors may affect the students' attitudes toward school and create an us against them mentality. Some experts feel that public school dollars would be better spent on books, staff training, and programs relating to peer mediation or other positive efforts, rather than expensive security measures. Nevertheless, some school officials feel that if a metal detector prevents even one gun from getting into their school, it has helped to reduce school violence.

Other actions that schools have taken to prevent violence are to eliminate places where weapons can be hidden and to ban devices used by drug dealers. Some districts have outlawed backpacks and book bags, or ruled that they must be transparent so that the contents are visible. Others have eliminated lockers. Some schools have banned pagers and portable telephones, as these are often used to set up drug deals. Some also prohibit vehicles with car phones from parking in school lots or on the streets surrounding the school.

The simple act of providing hall monitors, placing teachers or security officers at school entrances, or using television surveillance can reduce a perpetrator's ability to act without detection. Some schools have successfully used parents, grandparents, or retired people from the community to increase adult presence. Others have gone even further, using armed guards, patrol dogs, or police officers to secure the school. Communication tools such as intercoms or two-way radios can also help.

Gang Prevention

Another way school officials have tried to reduce violence is by restricting gang activity in the schools. The first step is often to ban gang-related clothing and hairstyles. This has raised the issue of whether these restrictions violate the students' freedom of speech. The Supreme Court has ruled that, although free speech is a constitutional right, obscenity, advocacy of imminent lawlessness, and fighting words are not protected. Some say that gang clothing communicates the potential for violence and that some of the messages carried by the clothing could be interpreted as "speech that advocates imminent lawlessness" because it provokes others through challenging words or symbols.

In *Tinker* v. *Des Moines Independent Community School District* (1969), the Court ruled that students do have a constitutional right to freedom of speech. However, the Court acknowledged the need to maintain discipline and minimize disruptions. According to this interpretation, if gang clothing interferes with the rights of other students, it can be restricted, but a gang problem must exist to justify the restrictions. The restrictions cannot be too broad (such as forbidding all clothing with logos) or discriminatory (such as enforcing a rule only against a particular ethnic group), and the regulations cannot be based upon a school official's personal preference or be designed to restrict religious or political expression.[14]

Some experts feel it is a mistake to ban gang-related clothing. They say that forcing students to follow rules they feel are unfair leads to frustration and anger and that their resentment will surface in other ways.[15] A more positive way to prevent vulnerable students from joining gangs may be to provide substitute activities that fulfill the young person's need for prestige, status, and self-esteem. Schools can also provide after-school and evening programs, welcome new students and help them adjust, provide solid role models, and develop a program of career counseling.[16] By keeping teens busy and building up their self-esteem, schools can keep students from being attracted to gang life.

Some schools have found that it is possible to take advantage of some of the positive features of gangs. Gang loyalty can sometimes be turned to the school's advantage by placing gang members in charge of graffiti removal, a school service club, or other activity. Key gang members often have strong leadership skills that can be channeled into positive activities. Gangs often have rigid ethical codes that can actually make gang members easier to deal with than students who are not in a gang. S. B. Hawk, a teacher who works with gang members, says, "They have the most ethical hearts in the world and they never lie to me. They tell me things I don't want to know. And if they think it will put me in danger, they don't tell me. But they never lie to me."[17]

Schools can guard against gangs by being on the alert for signs of gang activity, such as hand signals, disruptive behavior, graffiti, wearing of gang colors, body markings, and staking out territories. They can also train teachers in crisis intervention, build positive relationships with students, maintain discipline, keep outsiders off school property, and keep lines of communication open.

Teaching Nonviolence

Some schools teach students about violence as part of the curriculum—usually in health or social studies class. Students learn about how violence affects teenagers, how police officers can protect them, and how to manage conflict. They also learn how to handle anger and discuss how their attitudes relate to violence prevention.

Michael Williams, president of SAVE at West Charlotte High School, says that teaching nonviolence must start early. "For all of their childhood, young people are being bombarded with images of violence," he says.

> What we try to do is bombard them with nonviolent images. . . . We want to change the views of young people from thinking that violence is something that's glamorous and glorious to thinking that violence is something that is wrong. You can't solve your problems with violence.[18]

Members of SAVE go into schools to teach others. They conduct role-playing exercises in which they act out situations that could lead to violence, and then they show students other alternatives. For example, Williams goes through the cafeteria line or down the hall to show students that "if I bump into somebody, instead of violently reacting, I can say 'excuse me' and go on my way."[19]

Williams is on the right track, but is up against a tough problem. One of the most successful ways to avoid violence is to walk away from an angry confrontation, yet 52 percent of students in a national survey said that most people they know would say that it is almost impossible to walk away without fighting and 23 percent felt it shows weakness to apologize to someone.[20]

There is a difference between avoiding confrontation and being weak. A school in New York has a "peacemakers" program that encourages students to resolve conflicts aggressively but nonviolently. They learn to

Michael Williams, president of SAVE at West Charlotte High School, takes the message of nonviolence to youngsters throughout the area.

assert themselves by using the pronoun "I": "I want you to leave me alone" rather than, for example, "Get lost, butthead." Research shows that children who learn to assert themselves without verbal or physical violence are not only less likely to become bullies, but less likely to become victims of bullies.[21]

Some experts say that prevention has to start even before the child reaches school age. Terrie E. Moffitt, a psychologist at the University of Wisconsin-Madison who studied the connection between IQ and criminal behavior, suggests that funding public health programs that provide prenatal care and improve infant health would be the best way to prevent delinquency.[22] Parenting classes have also been named as an essential part of the solution. Deborah Prothrow-Stith says that "if all the children born in America learned at home how to manage anger and aggression non-violently, our homicide and assault rates would decline by 50 percent—maybe even 75 percent."[23]

Conflict Resolution and Peer Mediation

In the United States, five thousand elementary and secondary schools are teaching students how to resolve conflicts nonviolently. School administrators report that the programs seem to reduce the number of incidents at their schools. If nothing else, student communication skills improve and students learn to take responsibility for their behavior. Many programs work to establish basic values such as honesty, respect, responsibility, and working for the common good.

The fastest-growing type of conflict-resolution program is peer mediation. The process is usually conducted in secrecy to ensure confidentiality. Mediators are trained and supervised by faculty advisors and work in teams. They get students who are involved in a dispute to agree to some ground rules and give both parties a chance to explain how they feel about the situation. Mediators keep both sides talking until they agree on the nature of the problem. Then the mediators help the conflicting parties work out a balanced settlement that each side accepts as fair. They write up the settlement and have it signed by both sides. High school mediators may also mediate disputes between teachers and students.

The peer mediation system works best when it is in use for day-to-day conflicts, not just for serious incidents. By defusing anger early, potentially violent situations can be avoided before tensions have a chance to build. Peer mediation gets feelings out in the open, builds respect and empathy, and allows students to resolve problems themselves.[24]

S. B. Hawk started a conflict resolution program at Monroe High School in Los Angeles that used gang members as peer mediators. She hand-selected fifty-seven people out of three thousand students. "Basically, they're the leaders and the hard-core people," says Hawk. "I didn't select them because they were nice people; I selected them because they were not nice people." The gang members found that conflict resolution was to their advantage. "The drop out rate was tremendous. The death rate was tremendous. So they have found out that if they learn to play the game, or work within the system instead of outside the system, that they've gained respect."[25]

A turning point came when two friends, one a member of an African-American gang and the other a member of an Hispanic gang, got into a scuffle during a basketball game. "Before I knew it, they were calling in each other's sides," Hawk says. She took them into a closed auditorium. "There were probably 75 of them, half black, half Hispanic, and me," she says. "They were so damn mad," but they talked—for three hours. In the end, they decided it was just a disagreement between the two people that had gotten out of hand. In the meantime, the campus was roaring with rumors of trouble. So the students marched out into the middle of the school's quad, where everyone had gathered for lunch period. They lined up, African Americans on one side and Hispanics on the other, and as the assembled students stared in shock, they reached across and shook hands. That was a year and a half ago and there has not been an incident since. The students found out that mediation works and that they can solve their own problems.[26]

Gang members are now seen as mediators rather than troublemakers. "When the new kids come in . . . the older guys literally tell them that it's not cool to be violent," says Hawk. "It's not that you're a chicken . . . but you don't need to use violence in order to be respected." When Hawk first started working with the gangs, the solution to any disagreement was "let's go jump 'em," or "let's go kill 'em." Now they have learned how to solve problems by talking. Hawk says that their area has gone from having California's third-highest rate of violent deaths to being near the bottom of the list.[27]

Gang members like Carlos have learned to solve problems without violence. "I have a couple of home boys of mine that maybe two or three years ago, you know, they would have been shooting at me or whatever. . . . I got to know them better and they got to know me better. It's not about being in a gang no more." Carlos says gang members no longer bring weapons to school because they do not need them anymore.[28] Hawk says, "[school] is a safe place. They can go to class and get their education and they don't have to check their back."[29]

Some experts argue that making gang leaders mediators puts them on the same level as adult authority and gives them power they should not have. It may also appear to reward gang involvement. School officials have begun to worry about their liability in using students as mediators of potentially violent disputes. As a result, some restrict their use to elementary schools.[30]

Whole-school conflict resolution programs teach all students, not just peer mediators, how to handle conflict. Teachers support the program by educating students about conflict resolution and promoting tolerance and understanding of different racial and ethnic groups. These skills can benefit the students even after they graduate. Teachers and administrators often find the techniques useful for their own communications and in handling disputes among staff members or between parents and staff. One child even found the skills useful in helping her parents resolve a conflict between them.[31]

Many experts feel that teaching nonviolent skills could have a tremendous impact, not just on school violence but on violence in general. But early intervention appears to be critical. Schools cannot wait until the middle or upper school years if they want to prevent, rather than react to, problems.

Building Self-Esteem

Experts have found that when children are labeled as dumb, they tend to become dumb to meet the expectations of those in authority. Although this phenomenon holds true for children of all races, children who come from disadvantaged homes often start out with less confidence in themselves. When their doubts are reinforced by teachers who share their low expectations, the result is poor academic performance. Early childhood programs designed to enhance academic and intellectual performance can help reduce criminality. A notable success story is that of Jaime Escalante, of Garfield High School in Los Angeles, once a haven for gang members. Escalante's story was told in the movie *Stand and Deliver.* He taught advanced placement math, including calculus, to poor African-American and Hispanic kids. Each class began with warm-up music and hand clapping as students ceremonially dropped their homework into a basket. Advanced placement students got special T-shirts and satin jackets proclaiming their membership in the program. Escalante also worked on parents to get them to commit themselves to their children's education. As a result, 70 percent of the student body went to college.[32]

Amos N. Wilson feels that special schools exclusively for African-American male adolescents may be the answer. In *Understanding Black Adolescent Male Violence: Its*

SAVE members use skits and role-playing exercises to teach students
how to prevent violence.

Remediation and Prevention, he says that the standard American method of education is an instrument of EuroAmerican socioeconomic supremacy. Subjecting African-American adolescents, who are frequently the targets of white racism, to such a system is like killing them, according to Wilson. He describes programs that stress African cultural heritage and history, taught by African-American male instructors who serve as role models and who understand and empathize with their students. This exclusively male education and training is an ancient and honored tradition in African societies, says Wilson.[33] However, segregating groups of students prevents them from learning about each other. Such ignorance is what breeds prejudice and racism. The world is filled with different kinds of people, and children who have not learned how to interact in such a world may be greatly disadvantaged when, as adults, they must deal with people from different backgrounds.

Alternative Activities

If schools were always challenging, perhaps there would be less school crime, but as it is, many students are bored by school—either because the work is too hard or because it is too easy. Students then may seek other challenges—often illegal ones. One researcher went so far as to say that the wonder is not why some students commit crime, but why many do not.[34]

Experts think that some vandals just enjoy adventure; the more obstacles they need to overcome, the more challenging the action. To deal with this, they say, schools must increase the students' ability to structure their own activities and help them become motivated.[35] Schools can also provide substitute activities that give students the same kind of satisfaction they get from destruction.[36]

Do young people turn to crime out of boredom? Some researchers have noted that, particularly for middle and upper class students, the motive for school crime is not financial gain, but enjoyment. Students may view it as a form of play or as an exciting activity. Students seem to agree that boredom can lead to violence. In a national survey, 67 percent felt that there would be much less violence if there were more things for kids to do.[37]

Reacting

Although prevention is always preferable, when an incident occurs, school officials try to respond immediately to avoid further escalation. Particularly when racial disputes are involved, intervention must occur before a disagreement escalates, involves more people, greater force, and more dangerous consequences.

The most common reaction to school violence is suspension. The school takes the offending student out of class or out of school for a period of time. However, school officials have realized that spending time at home, unsupervised, watching TV and eating popcorn, is not much of a punishment. So some schools require that the student spend the suspension time at school, either after classes or on Saturdays. However, the most disruptive students often do not care whether they are suspended or not.

91

Even if the offender is arrested, the school may still have to deal with the offending student's return. Of young people arrested for violent crimes, two thirds receive probation or go free.[38] And chances are, the problems will not stop. The rate of recidivism, or repeat arrests, among violent youths is 70 percent.[39]

Counseling and Support

One way to reduce violence is to stop the cycle by offering counseling and support to young victims of violence. Children who are being abused can be removed from the violent situation and placed in a loving environment where they will learn that violence is not a necessary part of life. Kids who are victimized at school can be offered counseling, support, and protection so that the desire for revenge does not fuel additional violence.

Teen support groups can help those who are having difficulty getting through adolescence. Those who show signs of violent behavior can be given additional guidance and support. If necessary, mental health treatment can be sought. In this way, children will not continue to see violence as a natural expression of their anger, as an acceptable way of getting back at people, or as just a part of growing up.

If you ask an adult or a group of adults these days to pick one adjective to describe a young person, 99 percent of the time it's going to come out negative. Who's going to change this? It's going to be me.

—Michael Williams, president of SAVE, West Charlotte High School[1]

7

What Can You Do?

The statistics on school violence are alarming. Government representatives, researchers, school officials, community leaders, healthcare workers, parents, teachers, and law enforcement officers are all scrambling for solutions. What can teenagers do? Plenty.

Student-Led Programs

Experts say that student involvement is the key to creating and maintaining safe schools. In schools where students have no tolerance for crime, there is a greater chance that violent acts will be reported and that problems will be stopped—before they get out of control. Some schools offer cash rewards for accurate tips on weapons or drugs brought to school, while others have student patrols that watch for problems.[2]

Many students have gotten involved because they were tired of adults telling them what was wrong with them and trying to solve their problems for them. In a national survey, 27 percent of students felt that adults really do not care about what they think or how they feel.[3]

On February 14, 1994, students met at a National Student Town Meeting in Miami, Florida, to discuss the issue of teen violence. The students, tired of hearing adult "experts" discuss the subject, spoke out on what they felt needed to be done to reduce teen violence. They suggested cracking down on the sale of guns, opening up facilities where students could safely gather after school or at night, providing counseling to teens in trouble, and repealing teen curfews because, according to the students, they do not work. One student explained: "It's time to pay attention to and respect what we young people have to say." Sixteen-year-old Molly Moore added, "we can't rely solely on other people to make our world better, we need to do it ourselves. Once adult leaders see what we can do, they will treat us with respect."[4] Heather Thompson says:

> Look, we're the kids. We're the ones who see it, we experience it, we know who the drug dealers are, and we know who carries guns to school. Therefore it's our responsibility to stand up. We can't let political leaders make decisions for our generation because ultimately, we're the ones that have to deal with it.[5]

Organizations such as SAVE are another way for young people to get involved. Unlike other antiviolence groups, it is run by students, not adults. Gary Weart, who gave up his coaching job to help the students, acts strictly as an advisor.

> I think the beauty of it is that it was student initiated, it is student owned, and it is student led. I don't take over. I merely facilitate. I'm a catalyst. . . . I create opportunities for my young people to go out and do things and they absolutely amaze me. . . . I think most of the time, as adults, we try to do things *to* kids. But we never try to do things *with* kids. . . . This program empowers young people to be active and make a difference. . . . I think that's why this program has been successful. I've seen a lot of programs but I've never seen anything quite like this.[6]

Members of SAVE conduct assemblies, teach gun safety, hold rallies, and work to raise the public's level of awareness about school violence. Michael Williams says, "We try to prevent things before they happen. . . . We're not against intervention, we're not against punishment and prison, but I feel like education is a very big key because if we don't educate people—not just young people but *people*—about nonviolence . . . they're not going to learn it."[7] Gary Weart says the key is using peer pressure as a positive. "It's turning that peer pressure around and letting young people work on other young people," he says.[8]

A more direct way to get involved is to turn in students who carry guns to school, report violent incidents, and prevent violent acts *before* they happen. It angers Angie Bynum that people knew there would be trouble at the party where Alex Orange lost his life, but they chose not to tell anyone. Bynum says, "90 percent of the students know that something is going to happen and no one will say anything . . . it's getting better . . . but still a lot of young children are dying unnecessarily." She wants students to take back their rights from people who want to cause trouble.[9]

Protecting Yourself

Although most people, particularly those who have never been victimized, have an "it won't happen to me" attitude, it is wise to know how to protect yourself. Most crimes have four stages: surveillance, invitation, confrontation, and attack.[10] Understanding these stages can help you stay safe.

In the surveillance stage, a perpetrator watches the potential victim to judge whether he or she is a "good victim." A good victim has and will give the criminal what he or she wants, probably will not be able to iden- tify the criminal later, and does not see the criminal approaching. To prevent yourself from being selected as a victim, be observant. Do not be preoccupied with a book or listening to a headset. Avoid becoming incapaci- tated by alcohol or drugs. Do not call attention to yourself by carrying a lot of money, wearing expensive jewelry or clothes, or by bragging about your wealth. Imitation jewelry and copies of expensive clothing can fool criminals and invite trouble. Stay away from isolated areas, and if you sense danger, react immediately by run- ning away or seeking help.

The invitation phase is usually a harmless question such as "Do you have a match?" or "Can you tell me what time it is?" This is how criminals get victims to stop. Avoid becoming a victim by not stopping. Call out an answer without slowing down or act as if you did not hear. Remember, it is better to seem rude or be embarrassed than to become a crime victim.

In the confrontation phase, a request for help turns into a demand—usually for money or jewelry. At this stage, you may be able to call for help or run away.

During the attack phase, you may be facing a weapon and will be physically threatened. This is the most dangerous phase and one that should have been avoided by taking action sooner. Control your emotions; angry comments or refusing to comply can have deadly consequences. Move slowly and deliberately. Do not do anything you are not told to do. Avoid comments, actions, even looks that could provoke a violent reaction. Perpetrators are nervous, excited, and may be under the influence of drugs or alcohol. They have already decided to commit a crime—your reaction to them can influence the outcome. If you cannot easily get away, it is probably safer to comply with the perpetrator's demands, especially if a gun is involved.[11] One study found that one out of every four victims who used a gun to resist was injured. One in two who resisted without a weapon was injured. Of those who complied and did not resist, only one in twenty was injured.[12]

The same actions that are used to prevent other crimes can be used to prevent rape. If at all possible, you should try to get out of the situation before the actual attack begins. Avoid being taken to a remote location if possible. Attract attention or use a diversion—throw money or your purse at the attacker. Distract the rapist by talking; this could increase your chances of escaping. Sometimes saying you have a venereal disease or AIDS may scare off a rapist. Remember, anything you say that stops the attack or saves your life is the right thing to say.[13]

A more common situation for most students is being involved in a verbal confrontation with another student. The first sign of trouble is usually an insult or a threat. For some young people, such a challenge is hard to ignore. There are ways, however, to defuse explosive situations or walk away from a fight without looking like a wimp. Friends can help by saying something like: "Hey man, let's give this guy some time to chill out," which allows the person involved in the confrontation to save face. Or, the person involved can ask a nondefensive question such as "why would you say that?" or respond with humor as in "I know you can't be talking about me" rather than react violently to an insult.[14]

The key factors to remember in protecting yourself from crime and violence are to respect yourself, listen to your instincts, avoid becoming incapacitated by drugs or alcohol, be alert, use body language to look in control and confident, and ask for help if you need it.

A Look Toward the Future

Will violence in schools get worse? What, if anything, will be the effect of the government's increasing interest in law enforcement and penalization and its decreasing interest in social programs and rehabilitation?

Joe Kellman, cofounder of the Corporate/Community School in Chicago says, "Unless we fix our schools and give these kids opportunities, this current wave of violence will look like a picnic in comparison to the gangs and violence we will have in the future."[15] Kellman says that those in control show little interest in developing social supports because they are indifferent to the problem, or may even be unconcerned because victims are usually members of minority groups. Richard W. Riley, secretary of education of the United States, says that creating a supportive environment free of drugs and violence is a challenge, but it is also a necessity. He feels there are no simple solutions, and that law enforcement personnel, health and housing officials, business leaders, clergy, parents, young people, and school personnel all have roles to play.[16]

Most of the survivors of school violence mentioned in this book have gotten on with their lives. Angela, who was once in an abusive dating relationship, is now engaged to be married. Her fiance is a guy who once came to her aid when she was being beaten by her former boyfriend. She is in college and does volunteer work at a shelter for battered women.

Heather Thompson, who was angered by the way violent incidents were covered up in her affluent community, became a speaker and advisor for SAVE. Now in college, she founded the first university-level SAVE chapter in the country. She has put over one thousand hours of work into fighting violence.

Angie Bynum is now a mother. Her daughter's godmother is Dawne Orange, Alex's mother. Bynum works at a jail where she has to deal with young murderers. She always tells them about Alex. Although she relives her pain each time she tells the story, she tells it over and over again in hopes of preventing another tragedy. Bynum says, "The day I stop crying and it doesn't

Angie Bynum is now a mother but continues to remember Alex Orange and campaign against violence.

bother me and I don't still feel the same hurt I did the first day, that's when it's time for me to stop."[17]

SAVE has spread across the United States and to countries as far away as Zimbabwe. It is run by and for students and emphasizes peace, respect, justice, love, unity, and brotherhood. Members promote the message of nonviolence wherever they go. Their buttons and bumper stickers are orange, in memory of Alex. Coincidentally, shortly after the 1995 Oklahoma City bombing, Gary Weart received a prestigious national award for community service from President Bill Clinton. Weart said that the bombing made him renew his vow to work to stop senseless violence.

Gary Weart and the students who started SAVE console themselves with the fact that something good has come out of Alex's tragic death. Angie Bynum says, "One good thing is, out of all the children that have died, all the young teens and young adults, my friend didn't die in vain. We didn't accept his death." She worries that today's young people are getting tough-skinned. "It's going to be a sad world," she says, "when our kids begin to get used to going to funerals like they do to going to classes."[18]

Michael Williams feels that teens can change things.

We've lost so many young people to violence. We need to get out and we need to make a difference. We want to tell everybody "we don't want you to have to go through what we went through. . . . We want you to prevent it before it happens. We want you to make a difference. We want you to make a change. We want you to change people's attitudes and their perspectives and their behaviors. . . ."[19]

Gary Weart receives a national award for community service from President Bill Clinton.

Williams urges other schools to start a SAVE chapter to help fight violence.

> Even if you're not having problems. Start something. If not SAVE then something else. Start something. Because you need to take a stand against it. . . . Don't wait for something to happen before you do something about it. Do something *before* it happens.[20]

Williams feels confident about the future. "Yes, we're still going to have our problems, yes, we're still going to have racial disputes. Yes, we're still going to have violence, but we're making progress."[21]

Fifteen Ways to Help End Violence*

1. Support broad and comprehensive antiviolence public policy.
2. Assess and address the level of violence in your personal relationships.
3. Stand up against bigoted behavior or comments.
4. Welcome helpful community programs.
5. No longer use violent language, such as "I was so mad I could have killed him!"
6. Express intolerance for gangs, fighting, teasing, and drug and alcohol abuse.
7. Do not carry a gun.
8. Do not purchase violent games or toys.
9. Volunteer to mentor a child.
10. Inform others about SAVE.
11. Volunteer to help victims of violence.
12. Be a positive role model for others.
13. Learn about conflict resolution and anger management.
14. Raise awareness of the violence issue among peers.
15. Volunteer with programs offering positive alternatives to violence.

*Written by Heather Thompson, Students Against Violence Everywhere, Seattle, Washington. Used by permission.

Getting Help

If you are in a difficult situation and do not know where to turn, here are some free hot lines available to help you. Caring people can provide you with support, understanding, and direct intervention, if necessary.

National Victims Center (8:30 A.M.–6:00 P.M. EST):
800/FYI-CALL

Child Abuse Hotline (24 hours):
800/422-4453

WE TIP CRIMELINE (24 hours):
800/78-CRIME

National Runaway Switchboard (24 hours):
800/621-4000

North Carolina Center for the Prevention of School Violence:
800/299-6054

To report gun, gang, or drug activity (24 hours):
800/ATF-GUNS

Chapter Notes

Chapter 1

1. Dorothy Cheek, "America's Schools Experience Escalating Violence Among Students," *Nation's Cities Weekly* (February 7, 1994), p. 13.

2. Personal interview with Angela Bynum, May 6, 1995.

3. R. Craig Sautter, "Standing Up to Violence," *Phi Delta Kappan* (January 1995), pp. K1–K2.

4. Ibid. p. K2.

5. Ibid.

6. Ibid.

7. Chester L. Quarles, *Staying Safe at School* (Thousand Oaks, Calif.: Corwin Press, 1993), p. 5.

8. Sautter, p. K5.

9. Ibid.

10. Laura Kann et al., "Youth Risk Behavior Surveillance—United States, 1993," *Morbidity and Mortality Weekly Report*, vol. 44 (March 24, 1995), pp. 6–7.

11. Metropolitan Life Insurance Company, *Violence in America's Public Schools: The Family Perspective* (New York: Louis Harris and Associates, Inc., 1994), pp. 46–47.

12. Deborah Prothrow-Stith, "Building Violence Prevention into the Curriculum: A Physician-Administrator Applies a Public Health Model to Schools," *The School Administrator* (April 1994), p. 9.

13. "Serious Violence Touches 1 in 4 Schools, Study Says," *The Charlotte Observer* (November 2, 1994), p. 5A.

14. Kann et al., pp. 6–7.

15. Loren A. Evenrud, "Crime Victims and the Gang Subculture," *School Safety* (Spring 1993), pp. 28–29.

16. Quarles, p. 8.

17. Ibid.

18. Ibid. p. 2.

19. Chester L. Quarles, *School Violence: A Survival Guide for School Staff with Emphasis on Robbery, Rape, and Hostage Taking* (Washington, D.C.: National Education Association of the United States, 1989), p. 17.

20. Ibid. p. 18.

21. National School Boards Association, *Violence in the Schools: How America's School Boards are Safeguarding Our Children* (Alexandria, Va.: National School Boards Association, 1993), pp. 3–4.

22. Ibid.

23. Quarles, *Staying Safe at School*, pp. 4–5.

24. Personal interview with Angela Bynum, May 6, 1995.

Chapter 2

1. Bill Moyers, "What Can We Do About Violence?" (television special), PBS, 1995.

2. Terrence N. Tice, "Violence in Schools," *The Education Digest* (September 1994), p. 39.

3. Joan Newman and Graeme Newman, "Crime and Punishment in the Schooling Process: A Historical Analysis," in *Violence and Crime in the Schools*, eds. Keith Baker and Robert J. Rubel (Lexington, Mass.: Lexington Books, 1980), p. 9.

4. Arnold P. Goldstein, Berj Harootunian, and Jane Close Conoley, *Student Aggression: Prevention, Management, and Replacement Training* (New York: The Guilford Press, 1994), p. 8.

5. Shirley R. Lal, Dhyan Lal, and Charles M. Achilles, *Handbook on Gangs in Schools: Strategies to Reduce Gang-Related Activities* (Thousand Oaks, Calif.: Corwin Press, Inc., 1993), p. 20.

6. R. Craig Sautter, "Standing Up to Violence," *Phi Delta Kappan* (January 1995), p. K4.

7. Ibid.

8. Ibid. p. K5.

9. Ibid.

10. Gordon Bachus, "Violence Is No Stranger in Rural Schools," *The School Administrator* (April 1994), p. 19.

11. National School Boards Association, *Violence in the Schools: How America's School Boards Are Safeguarding Our Children* (Alexandria, Va.: National School Boards Association, 1993), p. 4.

12. Telephone interview with Heather Thompson, May 9, 1995.

13. Claire Safran, "Teachers Under Siege," *Redbook* (March 1994), p. 90.

14. Ibid. p. 93.

15. Joan L. Curcio and Patricia F. First, *Violence in the Schools: How to Proactively Prevent and Defuse It* (Newbury Park, Calif.: Corwin Press, Inc., 1993), p. 7.

16. Myriam Miedzian, *Boys Will Be Boys: Breaking the Link Between Masculinity and Violence* (New York: Doubleday, 1991), pp. 58–59.

17. Ibid.

109

18. Sautter, p. K7.

19. Safran, p. 93.

20. Deborah Prothrow-Stith with Michaele Weissman, *Deadly Consequences* (New York: HarperCollins Publishers, 1991), p. 47.

21. Miedzian, pp. 61–62.

22. Dan Shearer, "Defend, Argue, Confront and Attack," *School Safety* (Fall 1994), p. 23.

23. Mark I. Singer et al., *The Mental Health Consequences of Adolescents; Exposure to Violence* (Case Western Reserve University, 1994), pp. 22–25.

24. Telephone interview with Mark I. Singer, May 3, 1995.

25. Moyers, "What Can We Do About Violence?"

26. National School Boards Association, p. 7.

27. Prothrow-Stith with Weissman, p. 31.

28. Ibid. p. 34.

29. Sautter, p. K5.

30. Miedzian, p. 140.

31. Telephone interview with Peg Phillips, May 8, 1995.

32. Karl V. Hertz, "Wrong Signals About Violence," *The School Administrator* (April 1994), p. 36.

33. Metropolitan Life Insurance Company, *Violence in America's Public Schools: The Family Perspective* (New York: Louis Harris and Associates, Inc., 1994), p. 135.

34. Laura Kann et al., "Youth Risk Behavior Surveillance—United States, 1993," *Morbidity and Mortality Weekly Report*, vol. 44 (March 24, 1995), p. 11.

35. Chester L. Quarles, *Staying Safe at School* (Thousand Oaks, Calif.: Corwin Press, 1993), p. 43.

36. Lisa D. Bastian and Bruce M. Taylor, *School Crime: A National Crime Victimization Survey Report* (Washington, D.C.: U.S. Department of Justice, 1991), p. 5.

37. Prothrow-Stith with Weissman, p. 9.

38. Louis Rosen, "Violence Prevention: School's Newest Challenge," *School Safety Update* (Fall 1993), p. 10.

39. Quarles, p. 43.

40. Prothrow-Stith with Weissman, p. 9.

41. Moyers, "What Can We Do About Violence?"

42. Miedzian, p. 68.

43. Bruce Bower, "Criminal Intellects: Researchers Look at Why Lawbreakers Often Brandish Low IQs," *Science News*, vol. 147 (April 15, 1995), p. 232.

44. Ibid.

45. Sautter, p. K7.

46. Bower, p. 239.

47. Frederick K. Goodwin, "The Germs of Violence," *Newsweek*, letter (May 8, 1995), p. 16.

48. Miedzian, p. 67.

49. Ibid. pp. 64–65.

50. Prothrow-Stith with Weissman, p. 9.

51. Sautter, p. K7.

52. Geoffrey Cowley, "It's Time to Rethink Nature and Nurture," *Newsweek* (March 27, 1995), p. 53.

53. Sautter, p. K7.

Chapter 3

1. Joan L. Curcio and Patricia F. First, *Violence in the Schools: How to Proactively Prevent and Defuse It* (Newbury Park, Calif.: Corwin Press, Inc., 1993), p. 7.

2. Larry Gerber, "Gun Fatality Rocks Catholic School," *The Charlotte Observer* (January 26, 1995), p. 3A.

3. R. Craig Sautter, "Standing Up to Violence," *Phi Delta Kappan* (January 1995), p. K2.

4. Joseph B. Clough, "Solutions Without Guns," *School Safety* (Fall 1994), p. 29.

5. Center to Prevent Handgun Violence, "Gun Violence in Our Nation's Schools."

6. Mark I. Singer et al., *The Mental Health Consequences of Adolescents; Exposure to Violence* (Case Western Reserve University, 1994), p. 22.

7. Center to Prevent Handgun Violence, "Firearm Facts."

8. Laura Kann et al., "Youth Risk Behavior Surveillance—United States, 1993," *Morbidity and Mortality Weekly Report*, vol. 44 (March 24, 1995), pp. 6–7.

9. National School Boards Association, *Violence in the Schools: How America's School Boards Are Safeguarding Our Children* (Alexandria, Va.: National School Boards Association, 1993), p. 6.

10. Ibid. p. 3.

11. Center to Prevent Handgun Violence, *Caught in the Crossfire: A Report on Gun Violence in Our Nation's Schools* (Washington, D.C.: Center to Prevent Handgun Violence, 1990), p. 2.

12. Karen N. Peart, "Lessons in Survival," *Scholastic Update* (February 11, 1994), p. 17.

13. National School Boards Association, p. 9.

14. Louis Rosen, "Violence Prevention: School's Newest Challenge," *School Safety Update* (Fall 1993), p. 9.

15. Metropolitan Life Insurance Company, *Violence in America's Public Schools: The Family Perspective* (New York: Louis Harris and Associates, Inc., 1994), pp. 110, 115.

16. Aaron Epstein, "High Court Rejects Federal School Gun Law," *The Charlotte Observer* (April 27, 1995), p. 2A.

17. Bill Moyers, "What Can We Do About Violence?" (television special), PBS, 1995.

18. Center to Prevent Handgun Violence, *Caught in the Crossfire: A Report on Gun Violence in Our Nation's Schools,* p. 2.

19. Joseph B. Clough, "Solutions Without Guns," *School Safety* (Fall 1994), pp. 29–30.

20. Curcio, pp. 33–34.

21. Personal interview with Gary Weart, March 17, 1995.

22. Loren A. Evenrud, "Crime Victims and the Gang Subculture," *School Safety* (Spring 1993), pp. 28–29.

23. Shirley R. Lal, Dhyan Lal, and Charles M. Achilles, *Handbook on Gangs in Schools: Strategies to Reduce Gang-Related Activities* (Thousand Oaks, Calif.: Corwin Press, Inc., 1993), pp. 20–22.

24. Evenrud, p. 28.

25. Lal, Lal, and Achilles, pp. 21–22.

26. Telephone interview with Heather Thompson, May 9, 1995.

27. Telephone interview with S.B. Hawk, May 22, 1995.

28. Telephone interview with Carlos, May 22, 1995.

Chapter 4

1. Mark I. Singer et al., *The Mental Health Consequences of Adolescents; Exposure to Violence* (Case Western Reserve University, 1994), p. 60.

2. Terrence N. Tice, "Violence in Schools," *The Education Digest* (September 1994), p. 39.

3. Ibid.

4. Dan Olweus, "Bullying: Too Little Love, Too Much Freedom," *School Safety Update* (May 1994), pp. 1–4.

5. Ibid.

6. Ibid.

7. Deborah Prothrow-Stith with Michaele Weissman, *Deadly Consequences* (New York: HarperCollins Publishers, 1991), p. 6.

8. Amos N. Wilson, *Understanding Black Adolescent Male Violence: Its Remediation and Prevention* (New York: Afrikan World Infosystems, 1992), pp. 19–20.

9. Prothrow-Stith with Weissman, pp. 6–7.

10. Wilson, pp. 6, 11–16.

11. National School Boards Association, *Violence in the Schools: How America's School Boards Are Safeguarding Our Children* (Alexandria, Va.: National School Boards Association, 1993), p. 5.

12. Susan Banfield, *Ethnic Conflicts in Schools* (Springfield, N.J.: Enslow Publishers, Inc., 1995), p. 40.

13. Arnold P. Goldstein, Berj Harootunian and Jane Close Conoley, *Student Aggression: Prevention, Management, and Replacement Training* (New York: The Guilford Press, 1994), p. 9.

14. Banfield, p. 48.

15. Joan L. Curcio and Patricia F. First, *Violence in the Schools: How to Proactively Prevent and Defuse It* (Newbury Park, Calif.: Corwin Press, Inc., 1993), p. 29.

16. Banfield, p. 50.

17. Sarah J. Snider, "Crime and Disruption Among Appalachian Students: A Personal Response," in *Violence and Crime in the Schools*, eds. Keith Baker and Robert J. Rubel (Lexington, Mass.: Lexington Books, 1980), pp. 91–97.

18. Prothrow-Stith with Weissman, p. 179.

19. National Gay and Lesbian Task Force, *Anti-Gay/Lesbian Violence in 1994* (National Gay and Lesbian Task Force, 1995), Appendix F.

20. Anne Bryant, "Sexual Harassment in School Takes Its Toll," *USA Today* (March 1995), p. 41.

21. National School Boards Association, p. 5.

22. National Gay and Lesbian Task Force, p. 8.

23. Joyce Hunter and Robert Schaecher, "Stresses on Lesbian and Gay Adolescents in Schools," *Social Work in Education*, vol. 9 (Spring 1987), pp. 180–189.

24. National Gay and Lesbian Task Force, p. 4.

25. Personal interview with Tamara, April 12, 1995.

26. Personal interview with Donald, April 10, 1995.

27. Hunter and Schaecher, p. 184.

28. Paul Gibson, "Gay Male and Lesbian Youth Suicide," *Report of the Secretary's Task Force on Youth Suicide* (January 1989), pp. 110–142.

29. Personal interview with Donald, April 10, 1995.

30. Personal interview with Tamara, April 12, 1995.

31. Telephone interview with Angela, May 16, 1995.

32. Center to Prevent Handgun Violence, *Caught In The Crossfire: A Report On Gun Violence in Our Nation's Schools* (Washington, D.C.: Center to Prevent Handgun Violence, 1990), p. 5.

33. Andrea Parrot, *Coping With Date Rape & Acquaintance Rape* (New York: The Rosen Publishing Group, Inc., 1993), p. 19.

34. Chester L. Quarles, *Staying Safe at School* (Thousand Oaks, Calif.: Corwin Press, 1993), p. 68.

35. Henry R. Cellini, Barbara K. Schwartz, and Stuart Readio, "Child Sexual Abuse: An Administrator's Nightmare," *School Safety Update* (December 1993), pp. 1–4.

36. National School Boards Association, p. 5.

37. Singer, p. 22.

38. Telephone interview with Heather Thompson, May 9, 1995.

39. Telephone interview with Angela, May 16, 1995.

40. Parrot, p. 59.

41. Bryant, p. 41.

42. Ibid. p. 40.

43. Laura Kann et al., "Youth Risk Behavior Surveillance—United States, 1993," *Morbidity and Mortality Weekly Report*, vol. 44 (March 24, 1995), pp. 6–7.

44. U.S. Department of Health and Human Services, "Suicide Among Children, Adolescents, and Young Adults—United States, 1980–1992," *Morbidity and Mortality Weekly Report*, vol. 44 (April 21, 1995), pp. 289–291.

Chapter 5

1. Deborah Prothrow-Stith with Michaele Weissman, *Deadly Consequences* (New York: HarperCollins Publishers, 1991), p. 167.

2. Arnold P. Goldstein, Berj Harootunian, and Jane Close Conoley, *Student Aggression: Prevention, Management, and Replacement Training* (New York: The Guilford Press, 1994), pp. 8–9.

3. National School Boards Association, *Violence in the Schools: How America's School Boards Are Safeguarding Our Children* (Alexandria, Va.: National School Boards Association, 1993), p. 4.

4. James E. Boothe et al., "America's Schools Confront Violence," *USA Today* (January 1994), p. 34.

5. Goldstein, Harootunian, and Conoley, p. 8.

6. Alfred M. Bloch and Ruth Reinhardt Bloch, "Teachers—A New Endangered Species?," in *Violence and Crime in the Schools*, eds. Keith Baker and Robert J. Rubel (Lexington, Mass.: Lexington Books, 1980), pp. 81–89.

7. Personal interview with Gary Weart, March 17, 1995.

8. Goldstein, Harootunian, and Conoley, p. 11.

9. Vernon L. Allen and David B. Greenberger, "Aesthetic Theory, Perceived Control, and Social Identity: Toward an Understanding of Vandalism," in *Violence and Crime in the Schools*, eds. Keith Baker and Robert J. Rubel (Lexington, Mass.: Lexington Books, 1980), p. 194.

10. Richard F. Thaw II, "Preventable Property Damage: Vandalism and Beyond," in *Violence and Crime in the Schools*, eds. Keith Baker and Robert J. Rubel (Lexington, Mass.: Lexington Books, 1980), pp. 209–218.

11. Michael H. Ducey, "Vandalism in High Schools: An Exploratory Discussion," in *Violence and Crime in the Schools*, eds. Keith Baker and Robert J. Rubel (Lexington, Mass.: Lexington Books, 1980), pp. 229–241.

12. S.D. Vestermark, Jr., and Peter D. Blauvelt, "Understanding Vandalism," in *Violence and Crime in the Schools*, eds. Keith Baker and Robert J. Rubel (Lexington, Mass.: Lexington Books, 1980), pp. 181–192.

13. Ducey, pp. 238–240.

14. Anne Bryant, "Sexual Harassment in School Takes Its Toll," *USA Today* (March 1995), p. 41.

15. Henry R. Cellini, Barbara K. Schwartz, and Stuart Readio, "Child Sexual Abuse: An Administrator's Nightmare," *School Safety Update* (December 1993), pp. 1–4.

Chapter 6

1. R. Craig Sautter, "Standing Up to Violence," *Phi Delta Kappan* (January 1995), p. K6.

2. National School Boards Association, *Violence in the Schools: How America's School Boards Are Safeguarding Our Children* (Alexandria, Va.: National School Boards Association, 1993), p. 7.

3. Bernard James, "Metal Detectors vs. Student Rights," *School Safety Update* (Spring 1993), p. 32.

4. National School Safety Center, "Conducting Student Searches Under the Law," *School Safety Update* (November 1994), pp. 1–2.

5. Ibid. p. 3.

6. Vernon L. Allen and David B. Greenberger, "Aesthetic Theory, Perceived Control, and Social Identity: Toward an Understanding of Vandalism," in *Violence and Crime in the Schools*, eds. Keith Baker and Robert J. Rubel (Lexington, Mass.: Lexington Books, 1980), pp. 193–207.

7. Chester L. Quarles, *School Violence: A Survival Guide for School Staff with Emphasis on Robbery, Rape, and Hostage Taking* (Washington, D.C.: National Education Association of the United States, 1989), p. 10.

8. Bruce Hunter, "Making Schools Safer Than the Rest of Society," *The School Administrator* (April 1994), p. 33.

9. National School Boards Association, p. 9.

10. Sautter, p. K8.

11. Ibid.

12. National School Boards Association, p. 9.

13. Personal interview with Gary Weart, March 17, 1995.

14. "Restricting Gang Clothing in the Public Schools," *School Safety Update* (March 1994), pp. 1–4.

15. George Butterfield, "To Mediate or Not to Mediate?," *School Safety* (Fall 1994), p. 17.

16. Joan L. Curcio and Patricia F. First, *Violence in the Schools: How to Proactively Prevent and Defuse It* (Newbury Park, Calif.: Corwin Press, Inc., 1993), pp. 34–35.

17. Telephone interview with S.B. Hawk, May 22, 1995.

18. Personal interview with Michael Williams, April 6, 1995.

19. Ibid.

20. Metropolitan Life Insurance Company, *Violence in America's Public Schools: The Family Perspective* (New York: Louis Harris and Associates, Inc., 1994), p. 139.

21. Deborah Prothrow-Stith with Michaele Weissman, *Deadly Consequences* (New York: HarperCollins Publishers, 1991), p. 174.

22. Bruce Bower, "Criminal Intellects: Researchers Look at Why Lawbreakers Often Brandish Low IQs," *Science News*, vol. 147 (April 15, 1995), p. 233.

23. National School Boards Association, p. 5.

24. Kathleen K. Shepherd, "Stemming Conflict Through Peer Mediation," *The School Administrator* (April 1994), pp. 14–17.

25. Telephone interview with S.B. Hawk, May 22, 1995.

26. Ibid.

27. Ibid.

28. Telephone interview with Carlos, May 22, 1995.

29. Telephone interview with S.B. Hawk, May 22, 1995.

30. Butterfield, p. 15.

31. Shepherd, p. 17.

32. Prothrow-Stith with Weissman, pp. 168–169.

33. Amos N. Wilson, *Understanding Black Adolescent Male Violence: Its Remediation and Prevention* (New York: Afrikan World Infosystems, 1992), pp. 46–47.

34. Mihaly Csikszentmihalyi and Reed Larson, "Intrinsic Rewards in School Crime," in *Violence and Crime in the Schools*, eds. Keith Baker and Robert J. Rubel (Lexington, Mass.: Lexington Books, 1980), p. 186.

35. Ibid. p. 192.

36. Allen, p. 193–207.

37. Metropolitan Life Insurance Company, p. 139.

38. Sautter, p. K5.

39. Ibid.

Chapter 7

1. Personal interview with Michael Williams, April 6, 1995.

2. Chester L. Quarles, *Staying Safe at School* (Thousand Oaks, Calif.: Corwin Press, 1993).

3. Metropolitan Life Insurance Company, *Violence in America's Public Schools: The Family Perspective* (New York: Louis Harris and Associates, Inc., 1994), p. 139.

4. Steven Manning, "Hearing Your Voice," *Scholastic Update* (May 6, 1994), pp. 2–3.

5. Telephone interview with Heather Thompson, May 9, 1995.

6. Personal interview with Gary Weart, March 17, 1995.

7. Personal interview with Michael Williams, April 6, 1995.

8. Personal interview with Gary Weart, March 17, 1995.

9. Personal interview with Angela Bynum, May 6, 1995.

10. Quarles, pp. 60–78.

11. Ibid. pp. 60–78.

12. Chester L. Quarles, *School Violence: A Survival Guide for School Staff with Emphasis on Robbery, Rape, and Hostage Taking* (Washington, D.C.: National Education Association of the United States, 1989), p. 21.

13. Quarles, *Staying Safe at School,* pp. 70–72.

14. Deborah Prothrow-Stith with Michaele Weissman, *Deadly Consequences* (New York: HarperCollins Publishers, 1991), pp. 181–182.

15. R. Craig Sautter, "Standing Up to Violence," *Phi Delta Kappan* (January 1995), p. K6.

16. Richard W. Riley, "Curbing Youth Violence," *USA Today* (January 1994), pp. 36–38.

17. Personal interview with Angela Bynum, May 6, 1995.

18. Ibid.

19. Personal interview with Michael Williams, April 6, 1995.

20. Ibid.

21. Ibid.

Glossary

acquaintance rape—Forced sexual intercourse by a person the victim knows.

aggression—Hostile, injurious, or destructive behavior, often caused by frustration.

arson—The illegal burning of a building.

assault—A violent physical attack.

bullying—Intimidating or cruel behavior toward a weaker individual.

burglary—Breaking into a building with the intent to steal.

conflict resolution—Working together to prevent or settle disputes.

corporal punishment—Physical punishment, such as spanking.

date rape—Forced sexual intercourse in which the perpetrator is the victim's date.

domestic violence—Physical or mental violence by one or both partners in a relationship.

gang—A group of individuals, often from the same neighborhood or of the same racial, ethnic, or social background, who work together, often to perform illegal acts.

gay bashing—Verbally or physically attacking an individual who is thought to be homosexual.

hate crime—A crime against an individual, group, or institution because of its racial, ethnic, religious, or sexual orientation.

metal detector—A machine or device that can locate items made of metal. Used to identify individuals carrying guns, knives, or other metal weapons.

peer mediation—A method of resolving conflicts that uses individuals of the same age or background as the conflicting parties for facilitators.

perpetrator—The individual causing the action or crime.

robbery—Stealing items of value directly from the victim by violence or threat.

sexual assault—Forcing an individual to participate in sexual activities.

sexual harassment—Unwanted comments, touching, or intimidation of a sexual nature.

suicide—The deliberate taking of one's own life.

vandalism—The purposeful damaging or destroying of property.

Further Reading

Able, Deborah. *Hate Groups.* Springfield, N.J.: Enslow Publishers, Inc., 1995.

Banfield, Susan. *Ethnic Conflicts in Schools.* Springfield, N.J.: Enslow Publishers, Inc., 1995.

Oliver, Marilyn Tower. *Date Abuse.* Springfield, N.J.: Enslow Publishers, Inc., 1994.

———. *Gangs: Trouble in the Streets.* Springfield, N.J.: Enslow Publishers, Inc., 1995.

Thompson, Sharon Elaine. *Hate Groups.* San Diego: Lucent Books, 1994.

Index